GOOD GRIEF...PLEASE!

A DIALOGUE WITH DEATH AND LIFE

Tish Ince

Eye Publish Ewe

Book Cover by Tish Ince

ISBN: 979-8-9870259-2-5

ISBN: Ebook 979-8-9870259-3-2

1st edition 2022

Published by EyePublishEwe

PUBLISH

EYEPUBLISHEWE
PUBLISHING POETRY,
LITERATURE, ART, MUSIC
FOR HUMANITY'S SAKE
SAN FRANCISCO,U.S.A.
2020

Preface

These Days of Remembrance

'These days are nearing. These remembrance days and you are
wrapped up in a book.
This shroud of words that entombs you, entwines
you further into my heart,
vines that are now deep rooted.
Push me further still and I might fly.

David

· · · ● ● ● ● ● · ·

This Day - A poem by Tish Camp

This was the day I thought
was the worst of my life!
And it has proven to be just the first
in the life .... I now call my own ..
This was the day I will never forget
and have never been the same....
Since this day.
This was the day my heart chose,
To slowly begin it's own death ...
In the part he took with him.
My life thereafter, has been,
A sticking plaster,
On gaping wound,
And I am doing,
All I can to stop the bleed.

This day was the day ..
This day was the day,
My husband died and I,
Began to cry.

There are no plumbers that,
Can stop the flow,

No doctors that can sew,
The jagged tear,
No priests on prayer
To seal the soul-bare
Drip and wail,
Or tearing hair,
Nor music covering,
The beating rhythm of,
Fist against chest, or head,
or heart,
In his depart..

This day was a day,
No sun would shine,
Again as bright,
Or feeling light,
And awake at night.

This very day a very pain,
Began to live and flourish,
Deep inside - then deep no more,
Tears on tears & moreishly
As Amazon knock the door.
This day, a child soon to wed,
Has lost her mum,

At a hospice bed,
In snow and ice, & hunger fed,
In drink and smoke and days of dread.

To sit in silence, louder still,
Beat of panic, being ill,
This day took more away from me
and taking evermore since each,
A look at life around the web,
That I can,
Barely reach.

This day my bed,
my bed is where,
I stay to stop the bleeding,
If less I move, I see no fear,
And hearts still meet their fleeting.

Glimpse of life, if one awaits,
In 'somehow fashioning',
A limping leg, a final beg,
For all, encapsulating.
But this day, took much away from me,
In rooms, I watch life falter,
I have a widow tongue in me,

Now fear losing of the daughter.

So I will rue this very day and
Anger doth prevail,
In widow-mess I think is me,
In a heart that did not fail.

This day I learned that life without,
Is ever, ever, Ever, ever,
Ever, ever, Harder.

Tish Camp 28th May 2018

Facebook Life Event - 12th Dec 2017

Introduction

Good Grief...Please! A Dialogue with Death and Life

I am a widow of four years, seeking healing and still onward in my grief journey. I have experience as a person-centred counsellor, and I understand what should be happening, that I should *move* from one grief stage to the next. I should find closure, acceptance and a way forward in being without. Before my husband's death, I would have said, as a woman of science, well website and IT sciences, that this was the only method of good grief, good therapy, and good movement I should have expected would meet this aim. So, I was more than surprised when I began hearing my husband's voice three weeks after he died.

This book is a sweary account of *after-life marital arguments* with my late husband and his negotiations with me to re-engage with community. And that of my counselling experience, assessing my progress in this grief journey over four years after his death. My complicated grief, my upset and my life experiences of family grief and loss.

There is research undertaken on life after death and communication with our loved ones and how the bereaved have used these communications to support them in their healing process. This may be what I have done. We are expected to go through a process from start to finish that all the grief 'experts' believe we should. From Elizabeth Kubler Ross and the premise of the five stages of grief. To several psychological and theoretical, and philosophical beliefs.

·········

The after-life martial arguments? Well, they're just those of an average married life. You know? Every day things arise from questions or statements from a wife to a husband; 'Take the bins out,' did you pay for the house insurance? Are we OK? What are we watching on TV? Can I have the remote this time? And this family is a worry to me. What shall we do? There were arguments about sex and flirtations, appropriateness (time and place, darling), spending money, and what job I should do? The main area I was most surprised at was hearing my husband say it was time he moves on.

And that I should find another. Then his own confusion and how we both felt about that. His own conflicts (mine) with letting me (him) go. And maybe, just maybe, these are all my own self-talk – gestalt method, acting and methodologies. A chair method where he sat. No, sat *and* walked around. Left phones and wedding rings down the side of, and comforted me in. Where I was helped to get up.

How he stood with me when we went out. Walked with me to the shops and hospitals, on trains and buses, or in taxis. How he looked over my shoulder at computers, listened in on phone calls, Facebook messaging, watched me in kitchens, at gigs, in fields, down country lanes, under tree canopies, on stages, at rehearsals, when meeting men, any men, friends or otherwise and with all family events. And in these places, and at these times, answered me in my head. In the *as if.* The 'What would he say if he was here?' Both lead and supporting actor roles, the full cinematic view, in stereo, in the dark cinema of my mind.

·····•·•····

I was both an actor, director and editor. We (I) fought over the plot, screenplay and production of this widow's life. Even the cost, low budget, or if the pyrotechnics and lighting were effective. Hey, anything more than a white candle from Ikea would do me – and it did him OK. The widow's legs in mud scenes, and even if the authenticity of the colour of his ashes mixed in were a-typical. And a phoenix rising? Can't we just get a new Reiki cushion and some incense? No!

My life hereafter his thereafter was going to be more, for his sake *and* mine. Let's make Death and Life a project! Like a new build house. We can work out the cost, do some of the work ourselves *and* get people in for the areas we can't do or need a safety certificate for. It's not for leasing out to others. I'll be living in it, and when we're done, and there is just the snagging to do, you can invoice me (widow rates) and then be on your way! This was the plan we spoke about when he was living. And I assured him we could deal with his dying and my living after his death in this way. "Reiki clients, social media work, some crying, healing and I'll be alright, babes"...

·········

I suppose the main principle I'm trying to say here is it's with self-care autonomy. Yes, from our husbands (in our acceptance of their death) passed, we can still become without them. The attachments we have, as hard as this may sound and as difficult as this may be to realise, are to be merged within a new life. Particularly in dealing with guilt. Knowing this journey is a process. One that should happen. For us to be fulfilled. You know. Future lives alone or even with a new partner. To not be lost in grief. Stuck in grief and to know that you can do both and still honour them. Love them and have them within your hearts. Living. After their death. It is also a funny account I've allowed in my authentic true story to be brought to life in death.

·····•••••··

I expected to be a widow with a script that I could follow with ideas and ideals that would be met and firmly kept. It would be the way forward. Without stereotypes. In stillness and with wild howlings along the way. Until I understood that the last was given from my doorstep up to the stars and moon. I would weep into the earth, the snow, the sunshine, and into and through the wind. That my becoming against my own wishes would occur.

And FFS, please be advised I swear throughout.

Dedication and Thank you

To David for ten loving years, for teaching me to say
" I love you, and thank you for loving me." And for always
being there, even afterwards.

· · • • • • • • · ·

To my daughter Michelle, my grandchildren, Ellis, Amelie
and Franco, for all their years and helping me after he died
and for all the love and hugs.

· · • • • • • • · ·

And for my alive husband Dane, for his love, poetry, widow
tears, and for all the years to come.
I love you all.

Contents

Chapter One

Arguing with Death

"You said you would always be here!"

"No, I didn't."

"Didn't you? Well, I'm sure you did. When you married me, it was implicit!"

"No, I didn't, and no, it isn't."

"Alright, alright, alright!" (sobbing)

I wasn't sure who had the upper hand, who was right, in this ongoing marital argument, but I was cheated then at his death and cheated now in our talk about him dying. He is always gentle when he replies. I'm nearly always sobbing and angry, like an angry child told by their dad, 'No, you can't have another go on the big wheel.' Some funfair.

Fair? No, it isn't, no, it wasn't, and no, it will never feel fair or fun or any flippin' thing other than utter desolation and anger at what has happened. I know it does and did include a plentiful allowance to go on the roller-coaster, and throughout the previous 13 months, I rode that bastard ride every day against *my* wishes.

·····•·•·••····

I'm washing, I decide, at least a couple of times a week. I just see how I feel, at whatever time of day it comes upon me to *do* the right thing, make good of this dreadful situation. I offer allegiance to the fabulous hot water boiler we were so grateful for, paid for by an anonymous benefactor in our charitable fundraising before his beginning chemo. It was 4th January 2017 that it was fitted, and we were so grateful. I was so appreciative. He was safe and could stay clean and germ-free, with no infections and copious amounts of hot water. I watched him wash and made sure he was safe. I feel him watching me *not* wash and wondering when I'll feel the gratitude again.

"Yes, yes, I know... I will.... later today."

I sense him gently, trying to hold back a roll of the eyes heavenwards. The more he speaks with me, the stronger his judgements get, and then he trails off gently, reigning himself in a little when he feels he has overstepped the hurry-up-and-get-on-with-your-life mark.

"For fuck's sake! It's been 3 weeks! .... Please!! What do you expect?!?!......... Wait!"

He sits back on the bed. All that hovering around, trying to coax me from room to room. Me answering in a 'Yes, I'm getting to it, hunny' kinda voice. It's just too flippin' much! He's hurt.

"Oh, God! *You're* hurt?" I ask rhetorically.

I can't find the right underwear in the chest of drawers at the bottom of the bed. I feel like I've been mean and feel guilty all over again. Yes, I made promises when he died. 'I will honour you, your story, your love for your children, *will* get to them, I will collate everything. They *will* know everything.' And did I promise what I would do without him? Yes.... er...... yes. 'Don't worry, I'll not be a child grieving, feeling abandoned by mum and dad and everyone else in my life. I will be an adult woman grieving. I will be OK.' Lol. I will be OK. So, I lied. I thought I would be OK; I'm trying to be OK, but I'm not OK.

·····•·•····

"I called 'the man', 'the people.' Sorry, the insurance company. That home care thing I set up? The toilet cistern? Leaking all over the bathroom floor?"

"Ah yes, did you? ...Good."

I feel comforted by his reply, foresight, and momentary questioning of his directive. And my subsequent agreement with him. My 'okay-lets-just-go-with-this-he-must-know-something' gently criticised position.

"It's funny, I didn't think it was needed last night; it was only a few drips, OK, OK, a bit of a puddle, I suppose, but you were right, darling, I *did* need to call them. I just got up, and it's a right old soaking mess there now."

He looks gently smug. I feel both gently annoyed *and* taken care of. I'm smug too. It was *me* that set up the Homecare urgent repair thing. I know he found momentary fault with the expense of spending money on things that *he* felt weren't likely to be necessary. I get back into bed after flushing the broken toilet and waiting to see the extra damage I'm causing and pull the duvet over my shoulder, the edge of the heavy throw, grab the red love heart cushion and snuggle in facing the door with my back to him. I remember my point in the mini-argument I won a week earlier;

"No, darling, it *is* necessary; *you* are not here. Don't you get it? What am I expected to do, fix the house as well? Babes, yes, you *did* do all these things in the house, but without you, I can't. I *will* get stuck, and then I'll be all, 'who do I ring? Shit! You're not here; it's not happening, these engineers that don't wanna come out, 'job's too small love' and all that absolute, fucking shite we always got. Oh, sweetheart, I'm planning ahead. I can't take that kind of stress, not anymore."

He quietly agrees. I buy the Homecare urgent repair package. I want him to be pleased with me for thinking about the maintenance of the home. That I actually *was* doing something right in *my* capacity. He has to learn who *I* am now, all over again, the *new* me, without him. It's like a shock to him every time he sees or hears I'm not all able and ready to DIY, the hell outta this house and functioning well. A strong woman that he loved because I *did* do all that stuff before, badly, but at least I would have a go and yeah, he loved that. It's hard for us both, having to learn about each other. He is gentle with me when he does learn something about me that is now the new *norm*. He is upset that he knows he can't fix this very shit thing; I have to.

I turn quickly to say, "I love you," look at his picture, gently touch his pyjamas again, have a teeny smell of them, and turn back over again. I feel OK and loving towards him; he's gently waiting behind me. I close my eyes, knowing that's when I can *really* feel his arm around me. I let him move closer in.

"Ah, God, babe, I can feel the willy! Lol. Oh, goodness, one sec. I need a ciggie."

I get up, have a ciggie on the doorstep, come back and brush my teeth, as I always did. I don't want to breathe smoke on his memory too!

"Babes, my tummy is hurting still. So, let's just hug. Sorry, seems like nothing's changed there, then, huh? I'm still, 'please, one minute ', and you're all gently waiting for me. I love you."

I turn and stroke his pyjamas, trying to reassure him. Phew, he is.

"Yeah, I love you too," he says, hugging in.

·· • • • • • • • • ··

Days Later

He's got that 'sad look' again. Aggggghh, it's getting infuriating!

"Why can't you look nice and loving and just, oh, I dunno, there?!!

I say to myself, hoping he can't hear me; inside my thoughts, my brain, yes, my brain that hasn't got (I hope) a brain tumour.

"Fucking bastard brain tumour."

Yes, I will swear at that fucking thing. It *is* a bastard. It came and caused all kinds of shit in our lives, like a dodgy new friend that you *have* to let into your home for some stupid, unfathomable reason. Why would we let anything like this into our home? OUR home? A dodgy person that *had* to come, it's 'attached' to someone we love, and we *have to* fucking entertain it!

"Hey!!! Sit down. (bastard) Want a cuppa? (Bastard, bitch of a thing), Well, hey, aww, and, wow, you look so, er, er, well!"

Yes, that's because it *is* so fucking well!

·········

Trains

I'm crying inside, can't wait to get off this train and get to where the peace will reside, indoors. I've been able to hold it in all this flippin time, at my daughter's house, at my friend's houses, and now it's all just leaking out like the milk from the canvas bag over your shoulder. Cocky you were, putting it in without a plastic bag. Why? Why would you do that? It was five pence. Christ's sake; five pence? Yeah?

We do this shit because we think we're all OK and don't need any safety net like a crunchy, crinkly plastic bag inside our nice happy-go-lucky canvas shoulder bag, what we used to wear to festivals or weekend jaunts at the car boot sale. Yeah, *that* canvas bag. That fucking bag now has milk all down the back of my coat. I look stained in Cleopatra's bath wee! Phew, it subsides. Where the fuck did that come from? The sunset? The beautiful sunset? Yes, it was a moment of looking at something nice that I can't share, yet a-flippin-gain with him! Angry again.

"Aaaaand, there are dark clouds ahead, two furlongs to go, and it's the widow on the inside, coming up the straight. Can she make the bend? Is she? Can she? Ahh well, (pause of disinterest) Now, let's see and elsewhere, what silks are the other riders wearing?"

The internal commentator tries to sound like he gives a fuck, but both he and I know he doesn't. So, *the sunset*: one! What else? Come on! What else do I now *have* as a weird lady losing it trigger-on-a-train before I get home? Oh, there you go! Tea trolley comes around, and a rider in nice un-stained silks orders a raspberry cake thing with his tea. So, *raspberry*: two! **Raspberry:** Hubby has apparently patented, commissioned or otherwise claimed ownership of raspberry as his very own fruit... yeah? OK, what else you got? Coffee and shortbread (my order) *coffee* ... Coffee? Come on! I order

Twix too. Anything? Ooooh no, leave that; that one's mine. Any other triggers? Well, then fuck off till I get home. I'll shut my eyes then, all the bleedin' way! No, it's a shit journey, the first return from London of many, so set the boundaries, lady!

I'm home, having cried on the train from Bristol Parkway and up to the approach to Cheltenham, rang my daughter, cried a bit more to her and then gathered myself. I feel his hand in mine on the train just before I get off.

"Thank you..hu.hu...huuw," I blubber internally.

I walk across the platform and ask if the bus goes to Tewkesbury from here, in my little lost girl/adult, crying voice and am told it's quicker to wait for the train to Ashchurch. I'm directed with a ticket man's arm, to the right of the barriers, to the woman I can buy a ticket from. As I'm doing so, I see a fundraising stall about to pack up. The Samaritans.

"Ha... awww, thank you, Dave. Look at that, always there, finding me help, huh?"

I approach, put some money in the plastic collecting tin and see a woman who offers me a fundraising teabag. I spy the loose Quality Street chocolates in a medium, wicker basket and note my chat with myself on the train.

"Yeah? Well, I'm gonna have a rum and coke when I get in!"

I think, 'teabag' must be Dave's idea. I let him know.

"Ah, well, chocolate will do, hunny."

I speak about my crying on the train, and she helps. She lets me select the red Quality Street. She's eating one too. I'm eating mine, and it's a nice connection. She's covering her mouth, trying to be polite. I'm not, but just speaking and speaking and saying thanks and 'hey, the people on the Bereaved by a Brain Tumour Facebook Group are already telling me it's normal, and they go through this *empty house* grief too.' I take a couple of the cards she's offered and go have a coffee and a sandwich in the cafe opposite, whilst I wait for the last train.

········

I'm indoors in another 30 minutes and see letters on the mat, pick them up and walk into the rest of the house.

"Hi, babes!" Yikes, (the threatening smell hits) "Just taking this bin bag out."

I'm back in, opening letters and getting rum and cranberry juice ready (the coke bottle is empty on the side). The hallway seems sad of any people-ness, and I'm ready for a wee as I walk to the loo at the end of the corridor. I must change these knickers, I think, as they roll too easily down inside my leggings that fall sloppily around my knees. The nylon knickers, looser these days, were almost falling down on the way home.

I must eat a little more. Back into the bedroom, begin the off with everything and on with pyjama shorts routine and talking to him.

"So, yeah, I was crying a bit on the train."

"I know", he says gently.

"I felt your hand on the platform and the train, babes?"

"Yes, I know. I'm glad."

"It's so hard, hunny. I can really feel it. I'm sorry I sort of pushed it away. It feels so real. It's sort of a bit overwhelming... you know? While I'm in public."

He says nothing.

I fill the felt 'awkward silence' with me 'looking for stuff'; lighter, candles and the setting up of the pictures where I need them. The little 5 x 7 picture in its frame is on his bedside cupboard and is not well-lit there. I move it to mine. As I place it under the lamp, I notice his iPhone is not there.

"No, no? It's gotta be there." (gentle but clear rise of panic).

I grab the large, empty Galaxy Caramel wrapper obscuring the whole darn area and see nothing! More panic has now reached my chest and is making a clear course for my throat.

"No, no, no, no, no, no, no! (Moving quickly around the room) Sorry, sorry, sorry, babes. It's here, wait, one minute, wait."

Checking his bedside cabinet and opening the drawer. It's not there! But the Durex Play Pleasure Gel lube is. Stab!

Stomach! Pain in heart! Miss you! Miss sex! Our sex. Quickly *focus* reminder. Forget that. Look! The phone. Look for it!

"Oh no, no, no, I'm so sorry, babes, I must have it somewhere!"

I'm crying now, louder and louder. The front room, run. Sofa? Discarded clothes on sofa? No! Cosy fleece blanket? No! Tables? Desk in corner? Hallway? Piano top? Kitchen table? Back to bedroom? Spare room? No... No... No.... and no again. I fling myself on the bed, apologising and sobbing. I grab the red love heart cushion and bury my sobbing into that. I am so Truly, Madly, Deeply on it that, *that* even annoys me. I don't want snot on my red love heart cushion. I'm berating myself in front of him.

"I'm so stupid. I must have taken it out with me and lost it or had it stolen somewh..he..he..ere! Oh, My God! Why? So fucking Stupid!!!!!

My head is hurting, I'm crying so much, and there's not enough tissue for the black mascara, tears and snot. I grab his pyjamas and try to be gentle with them. I don't want them all crushed in my self-hate scene. He's touching my bare leg. I feel him.

"YES! Please help me calm down." I beg him.

He does what he always does: one hand on my bottom gently rubs and pats it, or rubs and pats. I feel comforted, a rising sexy, then full-on sad. I see his face on the pillow and fling my face into the edge of it. I feel his chest now and tell him.

"I can feel you, babes!!!!!!!!! "Darling, just hug me. (sobbing). I'm so sorry."

I'm snotty and sobbing, and he's all OK about that. He's just so fucking, perfectly nice and comforting, just letting me be whatever I need to be.

"I'm sorry I'm crying so flippin' loud! Your head! It must hurt your head."

He gently strokes my hair... implying, not anymore. I follow through with my hand on top of his. Grateful. So very, very grateful. The hair on his chest is warm and now wet with my tears. I feel a teeny bit horny while crying, then refocus on the hug. He likes my hair and strokes it so slowly. I'm calmer now. He's so good at this. So, so good. I'm gathering myself and just laying there.

"OK, sweetheart. I'll get up now. (Gentle sob) Thank you so much (sniff, sniff) my head's better now, (sniff, wipe) I'm gonna have a ciggie." (blow nose)

He lets me go. I love him so much. He always lets me go for a ciggie when I need it. I came back afterwards to the bedroom, where I'd left him.

"Babes?"

"Yeah," he replies calmly.

"Please...pl....ease, help me. Please help me find the phone if you can. Please help me, hunny. It's so important to me, and I'm so sorry I lost it. Please help me."

I get the tears rising again and feel the self-hate *stupid me* stuff coming back. I look in my bedside cabinet drawer as I'm sobbing. It's not there. I'm on the floor on my knees, crying into the carpet. Just crying and crying. My knee is hurting, but he's behind me, standing, watching my arse as I bend further down to search under the bed. Just watching but feeling horny himself.

I notice this in him and do a 'no-not-right-now-hunny-this-is-a-horn-free-moment' order, which I telepathically sent him from that very arse! Why do I forget that it never works physically? It has to have the "Oh, babes, leave-me-put-it-away" voice. I send the voice that he hears. Good! He corrects himself, diverting his gaze from my arse and looking respectfully, sorry, towards the dressing table and, much more convincingly, refocused on *looking* for the phone. I flick my hair sideways to get a good look (wtf, am I flirting? - come on, stop). It's there!!!! There it *is*!!!! Right in the middle of the floor, under the bed!

"Oh, my God! (sob). Oh my God, babes! Oh! Hu-oh,(sobbing) "Thank you! You helped me find it!"

I grab it and come out, sobbing and sobbing my heartfelt 'thank yous' to him. I'm slowly becoming *not* surprised whilst

I'm kneeling and sobbing, pawing the phone as he now looks a little awkwardly *sorry*, like his *good idea* had sort of backfired on him. Yes, *he'd* put it there! Right there, under the bed, in the very middle of the carpet! His *big idea*, letting me know *he* was there.

"I know you're there!"

I don't tell him off. I'm crying and too bloody grateful to do that, but he's every bit *more* sorry than he ever was and feeling the pain he's now caused. He's still standing, naughty boy apprehension in him, while I bring myself to my feet and sit back on the edge of the bed. He moves to touch my cheek to help with the tears. I feel his warm hand and hold it there a bit, trying to wipe the tissue quickly to catch any gunk about to hit his perfectly clean and warm hand. Such a stark contrast to how I look right now. He don't care how I look; he's just really, flippin' sorry. I'm forgiving, calming down and lay back on the bed in my almost foetal position, looking at his picture on the bedside table. I feel tired now and rest while he strokes my hair from my wet cheek. I plug in the phone charger, wait for it to fire up and beg the Universe and All That Is that he's left me a message.

Chapter Two

Missing you daily – Anger and everything else

I t's three more weeks, and I'm getting used to the early morning rituals: wake up, turn over, look at the unlit Valentine's Day picture of us with darkened tea light below, say

"I love you, babes,"

finally light the next candle and walk from room to room not knowing why I'm in each. I remember why as I get back into bed again, get up once more, and reach the kitchen. Fridge open, I stand and look at what I'm supposed to be eating. Yes, *supposed to be* because I don't actually *want* to eat, but he tells me I must.

"Yes, eat something", he gently encourages.

I reply harshly again.

"What? My body don't feel like anything. I don't want to eat,"

and then less harshly,

"OK, I will."

It's like I can't even tell him how I really feel and let the anger roll or the smashing of glasses against any fucking wall that I really want to do, as it would scare him. Fuck, it scares me! I don't want to make him dodge the ricocheted glasses or hear the twenty-decibel, howling screams he'll hear as I throw each one. So, I feign calmness as it's early morning, far too beautiful a day outside. I'd fuck that up for him too.

"OK, hun, I found some bread to make toast, and I'll do two scrambled eggs. That's good. Yeah?"

He agrees.

I sit down at the kitchen table in his chair. His A4 printed paper pic of him, resting, seated, head height, on the cool radiator. With plated eggs and my ginger and lemon herbal tea, I look up at the cupboards full of his. The organic every-things we ever tried to stop the fucking cancer. I can't look at them. The 'heal-me' brand lies on printed boxes of sad tea with no one to drink them on the open wooden shelves.

"That's what I'll do today."

I don't discuss it with him as he'll see them anyway. He can get over it. I don't want to see them! I go for my doorstep ciggie privately, leaving him sitting in the chair I left warm, waiting for me. I don't look at him when I'm back in and just pull the wooden IKEA step stool to reach the shelves. They all come down. Box after box. He walks off to another room. Good! I don't *need* to give an explanation. I don't *have* to gently *ask,*

"Is that OK, babes?"

Because it *is*, fucking OK, and *I* decided that!

"What's with all this 'gently asking' stuff as well?"

I ask myself.

"He's dead!"

"Yeah, but, come on, he's *dead.*"

My *other self* gently argues. The kind, loving, dead-husband-on-a-pedestal widow in the films, self. The she that can take all of this and still say *I love you* with every bit of her heart and wouldn't dream of throwing a tantrum, a glass or abuse at anyone and especially, especially, not at him. *She's* the widow he wants, I bet. He can take her. A righteous candle-lighting mistress that stays at home and gardens sweetly and holds his hands and is *so* grateful for every touch, every word, every smile he'd ever want to give her.

Not some bawling, crazy wife that pushes his ghosted hands away in public, that jumps out of bed to smoke instead of feeling his hardening cock behind her, that's now a fucked-up widow that wants to die too. Of embarrassment.

"Yeah, my hubby's willy. Yeah, I feel that. Yeah, we made love."

I offer that it's *in a dream* and maybe it is, but 'boy, it felt real'; I tell another lady that's lost. I don't speak of the hate myself porn wishing or the desperate searching for Netflix erotica of women and men our age whilst trying to touch myself and 'think of him' scenes. Less and less now. Too hard to do that and cry at the same time. The tears that would come as the memory of him would surround my hands, resting between my legs, and I'd choke and sit up to cry out loud. I stopped trying to think of him after that, and now, less and less, would I even search for, Sexflix, as the numbness in my heart has reached my clit. I know it will return one day, so I'm not worried. Just not right now. The feel of a man's arms around me is what is needed. I could emulate it's *him*, and that would be fucked up too. Passing predatory thoughts come and go. I let them flow.

·········

Hosptial Man

The doorbell rings 9am. Shite! The taxi to take me to the hospital! I see the driver walk back to his car and shout out to the back of his head, rushing back in, in my dressing gown, before he sees me.

"Two minutes, love,"

I fly around the house with yesterday's knickers inside out, work-out cut-down leggings, and a tee shirt with a sporty hoodie tied around my waist. I throw all my make-up into a different canvas bag, wet wipe my armpits and face and hide behind huge sunglasses as I get into the car. The Gloucester Royal Hospital, the last place he was treated for yet another seizure, is coming into view. I steady myself along the motorway earlier, noticing how the Classic FM track won't let me cry quiet, nervy tears in the back. I speak to the driver about the track and explain the next one feels like a funeral sad violin lament. So now I know that certain chords resonate with shutting me the fuck up in any tearful public ear-phoned bus journey in the future.

They know me, this firm. They all do. 'Poor Tish'. The woman who can't leave her front door unless adrenaline calls her for London grandkids or A&E makes me. Get over yourself, I say and 'fix up' for a ciggie outside in the twenty minutes I've got to go before the appointment. I put make-up on a tired face in some toilet after walking in avoidance of the main neuro ward route I would have taken on countless occasions.

I sit in the waiting area, flick the woman's mag and see the article 'my son was a monster with a brain tumour' jumping up at my heart and slapping me in the face. The tears start, and I'm gratefully saved by my name being called. The nurse takes me in, and I cry a little more as she weighs me, explaining, 'widow, hubby, brain tumour, article!' She understands.

I get into the room and don't care if I have cancer as the consultant tells me he's going to collect something or other from somewhere in my womb. I apologise to them all for the tears and fix up and try to sound like I give a fuck.

"My daughter says she's worried about cancer,"

I try to offer convincingly. I'm reassured it will be assessed, and

"We'll see if there's anything abnormal going on."

I'd explained all the bleeding loss during the year he was ill and how it started a month again after he died. I leave with an

"In time"

phrase from the kind but unknowing consultant, a more knowing nurse that says

"You learn to live with it in time,"

and my own numb-and-couldn't-care-less-almost state of play. I decide I still have some sadness to sit with, and Costa Coffee is calling. I'm about to sit down, and the man I glance at walks slowly, aimlessly. That slow, unassisted shuffle. That post-brain surgery walk. That cognitively impaired, sadness and I am transformed. I leave my sadness in the queue near the raspberry slices I was planning to eat and approach him.

"You alright, love? Do you have anyone with you?"

His 'looks like brain surgery' scar on his head invited me to help. He's alone trying to get back to his ward, wandering for a ciggie. The porters he'd stopped asking for a wheelchair, stick, or trolley to lie down on had rushed off, not taking time to see him slowly lift his arm to show his hospital armband after judging with advice about being

"Only for patients, mate."

Angered, I would rescue him and myself from that and *The Sadness.'* Sadness, that's now pissed off at me because it's now about to be served flippin cappuccino and cake. I ignore The Sadness.

"Fuck off right now. I'm helping someone. Someone that flippin needs it."

Sadness is more than pissed..good! I wheel him back. He wants a ciggie. (I do too) and we would have to go back passed the neuro route, the stand outside and cry and smoke alone route. The lifts and sad hospital shop in the Tower Block that I walked around crying in route when hubby was on the ward. The chapel route that I prayed in cried in and wailed in. Toilets that I lost it in. Yeah, that flippin route. That I have to now get over myself on because *this man*, not my dead hubby, this man was in need. No one else was approaching him, helping him, and I saw it as a sign to feel nothing more about me and my sadness and get on with life, humanity for others and public decency. It was also for my husband. For the wandering he'd ever or might have done alone there too. I told him this in the lift back up to his ward. Thankfully not the same ward. I wheeled him to his bed. I helped him again get his feet in and out and helped him steady himself just like I did my husband.

"Ahh, you're an angel," he'd said in the lift whilst we spoke. I offered,

"We've both been sent to help the other,"

and touched his shoulder with love. As he got up to get back into his bed, he stumbled a teeny bit trying to find his footing and, reaching out, offered me his hug. I steady him and accept. Feeling his love right back. His arms around me. My arms around him. The man's arms I'd wished for earlier. The Universe was listening.

· · · · ● · ● · · · ·

I don't go back to the Costa Coffee shop. Sadness has already left and is waiting for me at my bench, below the 8th-floor neuro ward I'd sit at, stealing time away from hubby. I have a takeaway cappuccino, bottled water and a half-eaten sandwich I'd just grabbed in the shop. Sadness is glad as he takes a little hold and tells me to let it flow. Hubby sits listening. Sadness is smugly stood drinking a latte.

"I'm sorry, my darling. I used to sit here trying to get away from you. You ringing me to see why I wasn't back on the ward."

The 8-hour days I sat on those wards with you. The 'just going a wee, getting a coffee, having a ciggie' respites to leave and cry days.

"I'm sorry I left you like that. I needed those moments to cry. And you, my poor, poor man waiting for me, needing me."

His sad aimless, ward-wandering without me moments.

"We walked here and sat here together. I walked with you here, babes, round the car park... you remember? Then I'd take you back and later back home, babes."

He's gentle again, offering forgiveness and thankfulness in his silence. I offer self-forgiveness in mine. In a moment or two, I leave, looking back once last to the sad place, the respite bench.

"I'm going, Dave. Are you coming?"

hoping he'd get up and follow. I was surprised to hear him reply,

"I'm with you."

As he was already standing right next to me, ready to help once more, to take *me* home. We walk like a healthy couple on a slow walk on a summer's day. I tell him I'm going to buy the man a walking stick and take it back to the ward. He thinks I'm getting over-involved. I get momentarily annoyed at him again but say,

"No, OK, I'll go to the PALS team and tell them about the poor man's porter thing."

The Patient Advice and Liason Service listen and know the wandering brain tumour-looking shuffle man, but take note. I explained my crashing through neuro ward anxiety experience, and they agreed that the brain tumour look-a-like man and I probably were meant to help each other too.

Chapter Three

Counselling

It became apparent that I needed to get counselling pronto. Three to four weeks of this? No way, I needed help. I decided to call a grief counselling service and, you know, take the plunge, asking for help for something I knew nobody could help with. My husband was dead. What were they going to do? But I just needed to talk to someone; I really did. The woman was OK, on the phone and listened to me intently as I explained exactly what I was feeling and how long this grief process was so far, the date my husband had died, the state I was in, and asked what they could offer. She said yes, we could help, and I felt so relieved. She began to take some details and then informed me that it would be a sixteen-week wait for counselling to begin.

"Sixteen weeks?" Sixteen weeks of this? Forget it! I'm sorry, sixteen weeks?"

She seemed taken aback, and I continued in complete disbelief and denial while begging for help. I explained that I was a counsellor and understood there could be something like crisis counselling. Because that's what I believed I was in. Then further, could they help with that? She pointedly advised me that they were volunteers, which is quite common and that the sixteen weeks were pretty usual. Indeed it's a small service that covers a broad region. I felt her at the time, what felt to me like hostility. I thought she was saying in her head,

"at least be bleedin' grateful."

I wasn't grateful. I wasn't making any allowances for the news she was telling me. I couldn't; I couldn't possibly accept this, just like his death. At some point in the call, I decided this was fruitless. I think earlier I did say.

"What if I was to ask my doctor to write a letter, like a referral? Would that help in any way? To show the need? "

Maybe, I don't know, there was a priority system of widows that were a) Really fucked, b) Half fucked, or c) Just about managing to get themselves back together again. Well, I knew I certainly was. I said goodbye, hung up and sat there feeling completely desolate without help. My next stage was to battle on regardless and see whether I could pull myself out of this. I know there are counselling services specific to grief and bereavement, and I was happy for anything at that stage. I didn't want to scare a counsellor with my tears. I'm sure they would have known and expected them, but I felt it would be a long haul, and maybe the sixteen-week waiting list was for us to go through sixteen weeks of crying. Ring out the tears and present with a slight drizzle, unlike the torrential rains I was in.

·········

No, as I said. No one can help. The person is dead. The tears are expected, and they will come and grab you whenever. Without a complete acceptance that tears will line your path, there is no way of getting through this. The members of the widows' bereavement group online are all thoroughly aware of how long counselling may take. They were entirely aware of how sure you have to be and how strong you have to be to go the distance, in the white sitting on the bench at a baseball game you don't wanna ever hit a ball at. We would repeatedly return in and out of this group. Check-in on one another. Assessing how far we've got in trying to find counsellors. Supporting each other with recommended books. Calling each other when we could and generally being online all hours of the day and night. This was a complete godsend. There were over 1000 members by the time I left the group a few months later. But before this time, it felt like I was a daily telephone caller.

There were times when this group. Really went the distance into the deep and darkest days and nights of widows and the bereaved. Us, clearing out cupboards and wardrobes. Managing to go to work, or not managing to go to work, coping with family, not coping with family, and assessing how we were daily. We benchmarked our progress amongst others that had been there for years. So I was angry. Angry at the brain tumour, I was angry at my membership of the brain tumour carers group and then angry at us all suffering such pain and for us having to be networked in such a traumatic way.

Earlier in the book, I got so angry about this, and now, as I come to the end of this chapter on counselling, in my retrospective mode, I can see just how essential this group was for me and for possibly every member of it. I am still in and out of this group, and we all seem to allow this in one another. Returning when we need to and supporting where we can. I've made some friends and lost some friends within this group, and I've had the wherewithal to support and manage this in the ways I do. This may be simply sharing Reiki music from a YouTube link with a few emoticon love hearts and that lovely purple one. Or, it could be me singing a song. At one time, I offered some music to others there, and

I remember singing karaoke songs on request from members of the group posting the video links or audio links for them to listen to or be comforted by. As a counsellor, I looked at these supports and the very different ways we as humans are so very socially connected.

Still, I would also now say we are psychologically, mentally and very emotionally connected during such a dramatic and traumatic period. This is amazing and shows the absolute human determination to survive though loved ones were lost, surviving the daily battle and wars that grief is. This is what is at hand here. There is no Joan of Arc leading us. But we know that we need to prepare for the battle ahead each and every single day. Some of us would be deeply wounded and still be cared for by the battle-wise. Some of us would learn how to dress our wounds, and others stood around shell-shocked. However, all were fed. We had safe succour and the opportunity to rest our heads on a bed made by those that were grief-stricken.

Chapter Four

Reiki

So, yes, Reiki was the way to go. I was to use this as my go-to every day to heal the gaping *grief war wounds* of *every day* and ensure I was fully genned up on all the glowing chakras. This was my go-to alternative walk around the counselling-blocked passage back to me. That sounds a bit shit, but (laughing) it wasn't. I'm not talking about being stuck like that, but I needed a movement, physically and spiritually. I needed *a movement* (roll of eyes). Yes, you too, reader. I am so potty-mouthed. I am so sorry. No, I really am not. I'm just... yes, well. OK, I'll go on. I had the Reiki cushions and Reiki clothes, baggy loose and multicoloured. I needed Reiki bracelets, more essential oils, music, and wide-open patio doors with chakra music on the PA.

I've never thought of myself as a hippie or a new-age gal, but I definitely liked this stuff, and when I saw my Reiki master for the first time, she was dressed 'normally'. You know, a loose white suit or blouse, a warm smile, and lovely bouncy hair. Ah, she was sweet, well-spoken and encouraging. I was 'cockney-in-the-country' in an apron and leggings. Hair in a hurt-me-hard bun and always smiling through the pain. The Reiki Master, who had met me a year earlier, helped me to help my husband, and then I joined the group at the Holistic Centre. Which was a great godsend for me and where I achieved my Reiki 1 certification. She then offered me a second opportunity to attend the Reiki 2 course. This would mean I could have people I could practice Reiki on. And that was wonderful. I set out to make this amazing Reiki room. I had Reiki music and essential oils every single day for myself. Providing myself with Reiki self-treatments.

The house was lifted, and the energy was pure. And any tears that did fall, I would soon cater for with these self-care moments. On the Reiki 2 course, I could have distant Reiki treatment and hands-on Reiki, and the following day was able to throw away my walking stick. Literally! I was doing knee squats in the kitchen and was totally amazed. So now my leg was working again. It was the heart, soul and spirit that I needed to mend. I continued with this daily.

·······

Vicars Gotta Vic

It was around this time. I had a return visit from a vicar. I was excited to show the vicar the benefits of Reiki and the fact that I was now, after ten years, not using a walking stick. The vicar was pleased but seemed a little perplexed, and I explained it was the Reiki 2 course I was on and the Reiki treatment I'd had. We discussed it for a while, and I was offered gently to come and use the church and told that if I did have some healing abilities, I should use that within the church setting and not, however, as a Reiki practitioner.

I was really upset to hear this, but I still needed and was glad of the vicar's company. I explained that I now had Reiki as part of my everyday life and used incense and essential oils. At one point, the vicar was quite concerned about this and prayed for me and placed their hands on me, almost like an exorcism, and convinced me that I should give it up and attend church and provide healing there. Eventually, I said yes, OK and goodbye.

I then telephoned my daughter and explained I'm now giving up Reiki altogether and likely to be doing healing through the church only. She was shocked. Then I contacted my next-door neighbour, a widow friend of mine. Explained that I was now giving up Reiki altogether and would be going to the church to use any ability I had with them.

Both asked me if that's what I really wanted to do, and I began getting upset and saying this was likely what I was expected to do. I don't want to do something *bad* in God's eyes, etcetera. But I was very distressed at hearing this and worrying that I ought to give up something I *knew* was good for me. My neighbour said. Quite frankly, Reiki has been the making of you. It's been the one thing that's kept you going. And likewise, my daughter said similar. More than upset and concerned about my ways forward, I decided to call the Reiki master. She said it's entirely up to you. Several different faiths may use Reiki from all other religions worldwide; indeed, there are a number of vicars that practice Reiki. Once I had heard that and led up these things online, I found that there was a way of holding both.

·· • • •• • • ··

Reiki Gotta Reiki

I then continued on the course, and things got wonderful. I bought some cute books and notepads to write in and found all of the key teachings, treatments and expectations through the Reiki Master and, finally, what was expected of me. This included finding people to offer Reiki to. That also became a wonderful story through the women and friends online on Facebook, the women at the local choir I attended, and friends on Facebook. Of course, I went straight back to the widows' group online and told everyone that I was now doing Reiki, and some people accepted a few online distant treatments and even in person. Gosh, us widows, lol. We really do the most amazing things. People really go the distance and try to help. I'd share reiki music from YouTube for those not sure about it or those who just like listening to calming and peaceful sounds. I'd post links into the group or with anyone who needed it on Facebook Messenger, Whatsapp or on a Facetime call. I was excited to offer Reiki to some of the women in the choir, too, even giving Reiki whilst *in* choir practice.

It is and has been the making of me and the balance and healing I needed from the everyday tears I was in. When my grandson came to stay, I was sad to say goodbye to the Reiki room but glad we were together and welcomed him living with me and for me to help him in his life. It was equally just as heartwarming to hear him say. 'Yes, I understand, Nan. We did it in school.' I asked him what he meant, and he said, 'I know about Chi and energy. We did it in a yoga session.' I was so impressed. So, of course, between his music, hip-hop, Garage and Grime music, the playlist most mornings would be a combination of these, rock and Reiki music.

·······

I've since found a combination of other music that has helped, too, including; chanting, mantras, Buddhist music, Indian music, and Tibetan Green Tara Mantra sounds. There are some that I sing every day. And all feel like they help heal the pain and loss and soothe the sadness. So now I'm in a house. A widow's house with a grandson, Reiki, Grime and rock music, a vicar that stopped calling and a knee that works. Let's move into the benefits of singing.

Chapter Five

From Reiki to Rock Choir

Yes, a Rock choir, believe it or not, will be my salvation in the first year, stage one of this grief journey. 'Sixteen weeks!' I said to her on the phone. This poor volunteer counsellor couldn't manage to gently tell me that there was no other way *but to wait* and wait for all these tears. Well, wait, I would not, I could not, and I was determined to find something to act as a sponge for the flood of tears I was in. I went straight onto Facebook to the local notice board for my area and typed in a post that would seem funny now, and it was then, but it's the only way I could manage to get across precisely what I needed. An advert:

'Widow: Early 50s. Social groups, activities day/evening for recent young widows? Think I really should get out a little. I really think my husband would want me to.'

I almost added. Previous good sense of humour! Would like to connect, along with something about counselling and helping to deal with loss or words to that effect.

I had a flurry of comments and supportive messages. People asked, 'do you want to go to this art group? or 'Hey, do you like knitting?' We also do crochet, and finally, somebody wrote, ' there's the local rock choir?' Yes, that's it! That's the one, and I immediately made connections by clicking the URL link they gave to the local rock choir. I looked at the information on their website, that it was held locally, and felt that I could, with determination and with him, walking by my side, walk right on in there and sit at the back to sing songs quietly. It was around £300 a year for attendance, which I feel was a pretty good deal at £30 a month to help with the counselling need that would have cost so much more had I gone private. And indeed, singing was my best method of dealing with all my previous heartaches and heartbreaks. So. Singing it was!

········•••····

I went along the first week, told people what my situation was, and was warmly welcomed. My intent was to sit, as I say, at the back and sing quietly, having sat at home singing the *sad songs* which I could no longer stand. I decided that singing in a group would be helpful and psychologically beneficial because at least that would be *with* people. The songs were an array of different ones, and indeed there were a couple that I just could not bear to sing, and people helped me through that too. Many times I took an *exit stage left,* outside, to have a cigarette to gather myself a little before coming in again, picking up the song sheets and battling on through. I sang so many songs that first week and felt uplifted to be with people again. The following week. I was no longer at the back and was asked to come and sit at the front. It was clear I was a bass, very loud and not as quiet as I'd thought. I was told by the choirmaster,

" Well, you're pretty short, so you'll have to stand at the front."

I took a spare seat up front and, in my bass tones, shared songs with other people who needed to sing for various reasons. But, we were at least a group of male, female, married, widowed, young, and old. It didn't matter. We had one task at hand, and that was to sing together!

·· · · •·•· · ··

Singing is perfect for several reasons. It's a great way of releasing energy, emotion, and feelings and, while grieving, using your lungs for something other than screaming. It was perfect for breathing in and out and walking there and back. Very good to do that. And not long after, people began to offer to take me or collect me and bring me back. Within a few weeks, the choirmaster had decided that my voice was good enough to try out one of the lead vocal parts and consider signing up for some of their shows, which I felt was too soon for me.

But I had a handful of song sheets I had to practice daily at home and make sure that my harmony was such that it would blend with everyone else. So this became a blended part of my life now. Widowed, grief-struck, but beginning to merge into a new life *with* the community, not alone.

·····•·•·•·••··

Of course, I spoke to Dave about this, and he was over the moon. There was plenty of

"Go on, girl!'

And plenty of me leaving the house wrapped up in scarves and warm gloves, saying,

"I'm going, Dave. Are you ready?"

He would walk alongside, listening to me singing along the road in case I'd forgotten some of my notes. It would not be long before I was singing a lead vocal part in my first show. Walking on Broken Glass by Annie Lennox and California Dreaming by the Mamas and Papas. The first show was outside the church I used to attend with my husband, which was quite challenging for me, but I loved the fact that I was singing there. I loved that that's where we were married, where his funeral was, and I was now standing outside, singing in joy. Other people from other local choirs across the counties joined, and it was something like 100 or more people singing altogether. I made new friends there and continue to be friends with them to this day.

·········

On the first Christmas in 2017, I could not attend the Christmas Carol choir shows; being the most challenging and most difficult time of year for many widows or the bereaved, so I took a back seat. Indeed, someone also got married, and the choir was asked to come and sing at that wedding. Again, if asked, I knew I couldn't attend. I just couldn't bring myself to sing and have reminders of my special day and my loss. But overall, the choir was everything I could have needed. We had a. I was asked to sing at a show raising money for a local hospice. I invited my daughter and grandchildren, who drove up from London, to sit in an audience and hear me sing. During the break, I went outside on the edge of the country lane next to a field, trying desperately to smoke a cigarette, and across the dark grasses, I said to Dave,

" I've done it, babes. I've done it. Look at me; I'm singing again."

Within seconds before I stubbed that cigarette out, I heard the call of blues music from a blues guitar played by someone on the edge of a farm, on the edge of another field. Floating across the darkened grasses towards me, almost as if he answered,

"Yes, I know, darling. Yes, I know. Well done."

At the show's end, we had great applause and raised lots of money for the hospice. I came off stage and cried with relief and a sense of achievement. This was a massive milestone I'd reached, and I will never forget that moment.

Chapter Six

The Front Room and Kitchen Sessions

Now the front room and kitchen sessions combine cooking, dancing *and* singing. Now we'll start with cooking. It was indeed the most significant task I would ever have to face regarding self-care; I would be yet to meet at the front of the cooker. The cooker, for me, had been a symbol of all things family. It was the essence of my womanhood, parenthood, grandparent-hood, and 'wifedom.'

· · · · · ● · ● · · · ·

Having been brought up in a family of seven, many times without enough money and food to go around in a single-parent household, food and cooking was not only the act of filling tummies, but it was also us children *being provided for*, against, at times, extreme poverty. My experience of food poverty as a child was clear to me when I would turn up at school looking forward to lunchtime. Or asking the school cook, like Oliver, for 'more please.'

So, by the time I had my own child and was *providing for* her, *i*t was imperative that I was able to do so with healthy, nutritious meals and a few luxury items thrown in. This generally meant; a big bowl of ice cream, a supermarket cake or something I'd cooked myself in the oven. As my career progressed, as a single parent, I ensured that food was something my daughter, her friends, myself, and any partner I was with would readily and always be available. I would pride myself on being able to cook, sometimes with very little in the house, but each meal was most definitely nutritious.

········

I wasn't used to eating so well when I met my husband. I wasn't used to not having to worry whether there was meat *or* vegetables together on the plate.

We were not rich, not by any means, and maintenance had still to be paid for at least two years after his divorce. So, food was a necessity and, indeed, not a luxury. However, we never went hungry. By the time my husband was sick, food was hugely expensive and organic to meet his needs. But this isn't about actual food and sustenance. I'm about to write more about how I felt *emotionally* about food.

In my early widowhood, it was all Haagen Dazs, Maltesers, Jack Daniels, noodles and protein cake. But I knew I would have to cook for myself again. I thought that cooking was going to be in the way I was used to. A return to that way of cooking and all that it meant for me. This was a massive loss for me.

·····•·•····

I now had to understand that I had become single effectively, just cooking for one. A single live on her own person, which I had never ever experienced in my life. From the age of sixteen, I always had been a parent, cooking for more than one. So there was a huge learning curve. When I *was* able to pick up potatoes, wondering how many do you have when you cook for one? I couldn't even work that out.

I remember calling my sister in Canada and asking her. She was very supportive and advised me accordingly. I asked about the regular practice of a single person coming home after work and whether it was OK to just eat sandwiches. Well, yes, it was OK. But that couldn't be a continued life in such a manner.

·········

I remember this stage. Recalling how my mother was. In her early grief. At my stepfather's death. And how her fridge looked somehow sparse and sad with ham, bread, butter, and maybe a jar of ginger jam. The frozen ready meals were plentiful, of course, but the expected onions, tomatoes, red, green and yellow peppers, fresh minced beef, and leftovers in Tupperware containers full of rice. Well, now, no more in her fridge after he had died in those early months. Now my fridge looked like hers. A protein cake, bread, peanut butter, maybe some eggs, and of course, ham. But this couldn't continue in this manner. There was a time when I felt like it was self-sabotage, and I was so angry with him for dying. So angry at the organic food that didn't cure him. Though I would not, and could not, offer myself the same good, nutritious foods. Oh, hell, that costs a lot of money, especially now I needed to save.

·········

So emotionally, food became another battleground of very gentle advances daily. I began with noodles in a saucepan and added some frozen mixed veg. I remember my daughter using an egg once or twice in a pan full of noodles, which looked nutritious. Each day, as I cared for myself more, I added more vegetables again, nothing too heavy. Physically heavy, I mean. The weight of a carrot would have a bearing on my soul. But a handful of emotionally manageable spinach would be thrown in the pan.

Sometimes I took photos of these foods. Plates of dinner. At *prescribed* dinner times, when I would have cooked for *him* when *he* walked in from work. Now, I was trying to do this for myself too. I would move into pasta, whole wheat, add some spinach, and maybe a tiny sliver of salmon, and I believed this was OK.

My daughter understood this was continuing for me and came up one weekend and asked me to cook them all a Chinese Curry. I panicked when she first asked me because I knew I would have to **cut things flippin up:** onions, maybe some pepper, and fresh chicken.

But I believe she did this because she knew I was having difficulty cooking for myself, and this would be an attempt at making me face the cooker, the saucepans and the life I once had. And could still have! After all, they needed their mother and grandmother back.

·········

As these days grew more and more, and of course, now that I was singing more and more, I needed the calories and sustenance became a regular thing. I was able to cook at least once a week. Before going to the choir, I'd maybe, have an egg sandwich or something that would keep me going. After the choir, I would have coffee and cake with the girls in the local theatre café, walk back, drink plenty of water whilst I was singing, return home for more singing and have a late afternoon lunch of some kind.

What I noticed was that I always tended to opt for comfort food, easy on the palate, easy on the tummy and easy on the hips. My regular shopping was now done at Morrisons, online, and I always made sure I had a Thai chicken curry or three in the freezer. But I would not survive just on ham sandwiches and peanut butter alone! After making that first Chinese meal for my daughter and grandkids on a weekend visit, I realised I could pick up the heavy wok and began making noodle dinners, pasta dinners, and all-in-together-fuck-it in the same pan, dinners. It would be a while before I attempted ever making a roast dinner again, but I definitely was on the right path.

········

Other things that happened in the kitchen, funny as it might seem, were my ways of engaging with people online, trying to remember the fun I had when cooking and waiting on my husband to return home from work. I had a Bluetooth speaker on a shelf blaring out loud music, and I'd be practising for the weekly choir with plenty of onions and chicken being chopped.

In between songs, I also uploaded photographs and did Facebook lives, dancing and singing for all to see. Now, this isn't unusual for me. When I had a *live* husband, I'd done funny things like this in the past, during weight loss programs riding my exercise bike, doing free weights and even a barbell once or twice or singing along to The Rolling Stones, much to my friends' amusement.

I also asked people what song requests they would have? And some people gave me high-energy numbers from Tina Turner, Aretha Franklin, Adele, Shirley Bassey and a range of others, all of which I did with relish on the side. I would be laughing, they would be laughing, and that's all that mattered. It was a good way of still engaging with people. My agoraphobia was such that it took a great deal of energy to get out of the house most days. My eyes were always on the doorstep, with the door or a window flung open, music blaring or trying to ride a bike to the local garage.

So, the kitchen became the place of the new me, without a family in it. But this was a place where I could still function, still find fun in. Dance around in, sing in and cook up a new life.

···•·•••··

The front room was a similar experience, but in the early days. I spent time singing, remembering that I used to sing there with my husband. Sometimes live on Facebook before he died. And then I'm in this weird and wanting Widowland. I found myself singing again, in darkened rooms, late at night, alone or accompanied by Jack and Daniel, drinking and singing sad songs. On my music page on Facebook, I had support from people who would try to help me sing less sad songs, and I'm grateful for that. But these, too, were songs I needed to sing. It's hard to maintain a happier disposition when they are still dead.

Generally, by the morning, I would hit the Reiki music, uplift myself again, get a shower, do my hair and make-up and ask Dave.

"Do I look nice?"

He would say,

"Well done."

Sometimes I uploaded lots of photos of me *looking nice* onto Facebook so that friends across the UK could check in and see visibly that I was OK, getting OK, and being OK. This didn't mean, however, that I didn't need a phone call. But, it was clear to me that I did need friends.

Chapter Seven

Friends –
Online, Widowed
& Marvellously
Depressed

F riends online are a godsend into the early hours of every morning. Or after difficult occasions in the early years of grief. And this may be all that anyone has. I remember saying to Dave two years before he died.

"I ought to make friends locally. To go and have a coffee with. Maybe go shopping? And just be connected."

We, of course, went out together as husband and wife and had associates and acquaintances every time we went to local karaoke bars in town. Dave had his blues music and blues gigs. And, of course, there were wives and girlfriends of his, musician friends, but no one that lived locally. And we rarely, if ever, visited one another's homes.

········

We went out occasionally, very rarely, to a local bar in Cheltenham for an open mic night, and I met two zany music kids who enjoyed me singing. And soon, we became Facebook friends. Kate (bass Player) and Robin (radical hip-hop skateboarding dude) were two such people, but meeting regularly at the venue was difficult as it was held on Sunday nights, and Dave had work the next day. So after he died, I found myself more or less utterly friendless in a local sense, that is, until a local widow, Becky made contact with me on Facebook.

It was wonderful to receive her message of support, and she took me under her widow's wing and offered me the opportunity to get out. We'd go for coffee or a drink in town. I was excited by this and agreed straight away. We went to the local bar where Dave and I would have been regulars and sat outside.

Within weeks, I met several of her friends, who welcomed me, but sometimes it was just too much, being in loud places and trying to find peace within myself when all I wanted to do was get up, go home and cry. Slowly and surely, I began to get out with another friend of hers, Carrie, and we ventured into town. We went into the local city centre, Gloucester, Worcester and, I believe, Cheltenham too.

These were the beginnings of making a new life for myself and engaging with the community. I had a rock choir and at least a couple of friends I could have coffee with, who would understand, this complex and challenging act of getting out and trying to be part of life.

·········

Another opportunity arose when I saw an advert on Facebook for an event with arts and crafts and coffee. As I said, I didn't drive, and transport would always be flippin hard to get around from a village to a town centre and partake in any activity, assessing maps and directions and travelling times, but I did. I went to the coffee and arts event, met the excellent and artistic Debbie, and we got chatting.

We had mutual friends who were musicians and playing locally at a pub called the Frog and Fiddle. We agreed to meet, and **I went on my own on a bus** that dropped me right outside. It was a reggae band that my husband knew the lead singer of (Kingsley Salmon) and had even taught him blues chords back in the day.

It was just about OK. To be standing there, in a place me and my husband would have enjoyed on any typical weekend.

I managed to stay for the night and then get the last bus home. Of course, I was scared about being out at night, but I knew that Dave sat with me on that bus and walked me back to the front door, so I felt safe. Debbie and I continue to be friends and go to different activities that are held locally.

·····●·●·····

At some point, my hip-hop friend Robin made contact and said he had a gig at a local festival. So, we arranged to go together. It was great to be in such a place as Dave, and I used to go to blues festivals together. This local festival was called Dave Fest, and that was the very reason that I attended.

My friend had Technical difficulties with his media equipment before he did his gig and asked me for help.

Standing in the crowd of hippies and loved-up festival people, I did the only thing *I knew*, to help. I jumped on stage and spoke to the audience, telling them this was for Dave, that I'm widowed and started singing Aretha Franklin.

When Robin, my hip-hop friend, had sorted his technical problems, the crowds applauded me and asked if that was the truth. I said

"Yes, I'm widowed recently, his name was/is Dave, and that's why I came to this fest. Because it's called Dave".

It was another achievement and nod to my husband, show-ing him,

"Look, I'm still doing OK, darling."

I got the taxi home at the Cinderella hours I was offered, 9:30 PM and told him all about it when I got in. My artsy friend Debbie also saw me at the festival and shouted,

"Tish!" It was a moment of pure joy for me.

I felt like I'd been missed and wanted. She hugged me so much, and all the aloneness fell immediately away. Robin is my friend and was then and is now an exceptional person, neuro-diverse and uplifting to the max to all those who need it!

·· • • • • • • ··

Jackie, on Facebook, knew me before he died, met me at a comedy arts thing in a Gloucester pub on my engagement and sat and drank with me for a whole afternoon, apparently. This is funny. I don't recall much as I was flying high then on the love thing,

"I'm engaged" for fuck sake, I'm engaged!"

And probably too shit-faced to remember her, but she re-minded me that we had and seeing as I couldn't see any photos of her in my skimming her Facebook profile, I took her word

for it. Over ten years of friendship with someone whose face
you can't recall? Ha ha, what the hell is that, Tish? We nearly
did meet at the Last Blues festival my husband lived for, and
yet she was like the scarlet flippin pimpernel, and I was always
grateful for the 'where were you?' updates on her profile page.

She is funny, and so am I, and we clicked like girls in school.
The ones that get chucked out from the back of the class.
She was there, with others with a 'history' with us, to boost
us with all the cancer treatment for him. She'd send love and
love hearts and kept us in hers when the blue ambulance
lights were flashing, and then after, in my widow days, was
the online friend that checked in on me through Facebook,
boosting me in my poetry and ever since on WhatsApp and
during the Lockdown.

She does stuff, just knows stuff and is political and heartfelt
for all kinds of causes and people, and when my poetry began,
she and Sammich Man were the two most important people
encouraging me to go on. She is terrific at listening and helping through anything family or woman things 'I'm putting
on weight, erm, fuck it. Let's eat green'; what writing stuff
shall we do during Lockdown. We even arranged an online
campaign raising money for PPE across our county hospitals.
None of us can sew, for flip's sake, but we did it.

I would work anywhere with this woman. She is determined and funny and precise, and loving and understands

dreams. She writes the most amazing dreams and books in the making, is a writer and a poet, and I dearly love her to the moon and back.

·············

Keren is a wonderful friend and feminist. A supporter of the downtrodden, politicised and uplifter of widows. She supported me through every part of my written and verbal story. Coffees, online phone calls, poetry and just her continued ongoing support. She's been absolutely incredible, and I can't say thank you enough for every single connection with me. It has lifted me so much, and I'm happy she has been connected to me online in poetry groups, coming along to Zoom poetry readings and just being there at the end of the phone. Or with a lovely gif or love heart image that she sends or posts on WhatsApp or Facebook.

Every single one has lifted me or kept me going. Every comment she's ever said about my writing, like, 'This is wonderful, Tish. Oh, you can really feel it,' has profoundly boosted me. Along with everyone else's comments, it's meant so much more to me and knowing her through poetry and through friends, it's been just so good to be grateful for this beautiful, exceptionally supportive friendship. Thank you for being

there. Thank you so much for listening to everything. I love
you.

· · • • • • • • · ·

Wendy and Nik from the bereavement group were fantastic.
Wendy was so supportive. She came to my house and stayed
when I couldn't cope with family stuff and general loneliness
and gave me tips on early widowhood that I learned would
ease the pain, like,

"So what about the dishes? If you get paper plates, they just
go in the bin."

Ah ha! That's a great idea. I saw this in action with my
widowed husband when he was doing the same. We now eat
on plates and still have to do the washing up. Wendy invited
me to her caravan, and I was at a disco with her, drinking
widow cocktails, swimming in the pool, and having a shared
get-lost-we're-widows holiday together. She let me do Reiki
on her at my home and helped me have a girls' night in, full
of easy-on-the-tummy food, a bottle of something fruit cider,
I think, and talks into the night about our lost husbands and
new lives we were trying to make.

· · • • • • • • · ·

Nik was a member of the bereavement group, too and was also into Reiki. Again funny and supportive in our dark grief humour when crying was too darn flippin much, but she was always the reiki widow healer I needed, even with the little rainbow emoticons that we both knew meant Reiki.

She loved music and was pleased when I sang her favourite David Bowie song, 'We Can Be Heroes' online at Smule karaoke and for my sharing clips with her. I nearly went to meet her in the middle of the UK, but again didn't drive and didn't do the crying trains alone. Sadly, I'm now in San Francisco, but we are still connected, and even in spirit, I send her my love.

·········

Vickie was a friend from the choir, and she, too, befriended me and took me under her wing. Whatsapping and calls supported us both. I ended up staying at her house, going for drinks in Upton, near where the Upton Blues Festival is held and taking my first outdoor selfies with a mate. You may even see us dancing together on my TikTok profile. She had lost too, and we were dancing through all our griefs.

·········

The bereavement group online was also where people arranged to meet up and would find a fantastic amount of support from one another. And some groups do try to do this regularly. So it isn't all support group talk. It's also 'make a life again' talk and the act of making that happen. I remember once we talked about having a widows disco. Which would be really encouraging for us; with every step we took, every two-step shuffle or the bump, or dancing along to Saturday night fever, would have come from the bottom of our boots. Widow boots. Widow pain. We could dance and uplift one another, knowing that these were our Cinderella Balls and that no Prince would come, that we would return to our empty homes and probably more tears.

There was a time when I got dressed up. I sound surprised, but I never believed I would again, but I did go to the choir's Christmas Ball. I danced and sang and laughed all night. Except when I went outside for a ciggie, telling Dave,

"I'm doing it, for fucks sake. Look at me doing it."

It was good being with people that knew my story.

· • • • • • • • · ·

It was always tricky to be in a group of people who were not widowed, bereaved, or had experienced such loss, or didn't know that I was widowed. There's an expectation we have of others that they may be just a wee bit more gentle once they understand our story. Just a little less loud, and this is hard for others that don't know Widowland or what the Kingdom of Grief looks like. As they are simply *living* their lives and asking *you* to join them.

To do so with all authenticity would mean bringing tears, sitting on chairs you can hardly move from, politely refusing to get on a karaoke mic, and not being able to dance up the front of the stage at a gig. It will mean refusing to go to or stay at a raucous party and jostling at any bar in town.

It is so very hard. And it is not their fault or yours, but you need to be gentle with yourself during this time and not expect yourself to be anything like you may have been before they died.

So, of course, because of this, there are often refusals. This doesn't mean. That you don't want to connect. It just means that right now, it's so tough.

And there are days and times throughout any day that you may have the ability to just get up and sing, to just get up and dance, but it has to come in the small measures that **you** allow yourself.

·········

In this tender and fragile time, nothing should be rushed, nothing should be forced, and certainly, no one should push you further than you believe you should go.

Notwithstanding, you should not refuse every single thing, but make a plan to find the strength to attend, to be part of life. Ensure you can leave early if you need to and get safely back home. Saying to yourself,

"Well done. Well done, girl. Well done."

··•••••••··

Tracey, Annabel and Richard are friends from my student days, counselling friends who were very supportive when he was sick and died. Again, a special bunch of people that knew all the history and were either on WhatsApp calls or emails or Facebook or visiting or sending flowers, love and cards. I slowly grew less able to call many people as I felt the depth of these despairs was too much for those warm people in their homes or with their families. It was just too much and would have been too needful. I had to do this with others that were or had been widowed, had lost someone to the same deadly brain tumour or were possibly within reach walk to a coffee bar friends. Sadly, we lost Richard this year, and I have written poetry for him, too. We are feeling this terribly as we were the little gang at Uni. We did crazy things like book a recording studio for my birthday to sing songs all day, dancing at discos, helping me find a man when I was turning straight, countless nights in pubs, at each other's houses and sadly again, at funerals.

· · • • • • • · · ·

Other friends you may have had before your loved one died will also be a godsend, especially if they live locally. If they don't and you can drive, go see them. Stay with them, and be gentle with yourself. Get the hugs you need, the comfort food they make and the telephone calls that keep you connected. Sometimes this is very hard. If they equally have families, cookers full of food, and husbands alive that are waiting to eat.

These are difficult things to view and be part of; witnessing their friendship, being a lover, a woman and her husband, her family, and children. But the remembrance of all the love they gave you before, during and after your husband's death should be a comfort. I had a few friends in different places across the UK and, again, found it hard to travel on trains and had to contact them mainly on Facebook. Which is still a wonderful thing.

· · • • • • • · · ·

I noticed that I regarded the presence of **The Widowed, Bereaved or Marvellously Depressed;** we're people I could spend time with easily. They had a great deal in common with me and equally may have had difficulty in some of the same scenarios I've just mentioned above.

They would be able to understand the 'gotta go' and the 'just can't make it' statements and would still offer love and support in many other ways. You can make a life with friends from the ashes of the one before. It is doable, even without any. Be open to all new people and especially so, the bereaved. I made new friends through the poetry society I was a member of and was courageous enough to get to poetry open mic events, sometimes on my own.

I noticed that my Facebook friends, or those I barely met enough in person over the years that may have known me, some for ten years or more, were a constant support throughout his sickness and death.

········

And, in my widowhood, people have willed me on to greater participation in life. Sometimes these things were not even discussed, but each time I posted something crazy I was doing, like a women's DJing course three to four months after he died, they would put great big love hearts over each thing.

These little emoticons were so encouraging for me, every single one. Every single time.

Like being on a lost raft, over the water. I was always floating in a lake that had a warm and sandy beach to bounce around in, even if I couldn't easily disembark.

Friends were everything I needed, and whether widowed, marvellously depressed or not, I knew that that would be the bridge between the ash he was in or **the-after-life** I would take. These people gave their all when I had none and are loved.

Chapter Eight

His Clothes – His Things and a Flood

His Clothes - 29/2/2020

Today was the day. I should've been on the playwriting course 'Playwriting Adaptation' with Go Write in Somerset, where David was born. I didn't go, couldn't go, because I had planned for today to be the day I would bag up his clothes to take to the Sue Ryder charity shop.

My daughter agreed she would be available on Monday, and my grandson would be helping me to lift and carry the bags I filled, ready for her to collect. It was supposed to be a practical exercise to create more space for my belongings after decorating my grandson's bedroom.

I emptied out the fitted wardrobe of Dave's gigging equipment and was now overwhelmed with the very essence of Dave all around me in the living room. Clearing his clothes from the pine wardrobe in my bedroom was stage one of freeing up space for me. The double-fitted wardrobe next to mine was also filled with Dave's things. I remember building shelves in mine to put away my clothes.

This was around May or June 2018, 6 months after his death, because back then, I was still surrounded by Dave's things on his side of the bed. I couldn't bear opening the door of his wardrobe. Every time I did, I would throw my face into the softest T-shirts and the thickest jumpers that may have held his smell. Tears would be streaming down my face, and I would be catching my breath and hanging onto those hangers. Inevitably, I would close the wardrobe door quickly in a vain effort to trap his smell for emergency use. I met a man a month later and never opened that door again.

········

Some might say I should've gotten rid of the clothes as soon as he died. Maybe that was right, but for me on my own, in this house, his T-shirts, pyjamas and a stroke of his coat on the back of the kitchen door would be as much a comfort as it would later be a hindrance to me moving on, into the acceptance of his death. People mentioned *doing the clothes*, but I could never really manage it. Initially, I didn't have transport, and when I did, I was too much of a mess to tackle this.

There were problems in the relationship with the man, and I began to need to see David's coat on the back of the door, touch it, and hug myself with it when I was upset and alone.

"You'll look after me, won't you?" I'd sob

after another door-slamming 'goodbye row' with the man. He'd stay silent.

"I trust you. Babes, please make sure I'm OK," breathing quickly,

sitting decidedly next to Dave's picture on the radiator and looking at our first smiling, hugging photo together, stuck by magnets to the fridge.

He'd smile back at me, and I would calm. the man would calm, and I was so grateful every time he came back. I knew, though, that I still might need David's clothes. I wasn't quite ready, wasn't quite strong enough yet, to let them go. The man later went, and I began to get strong again, and now, right here and now, this was the day, the very day I was strong enough and would complete. Two years, two months and two weeks after his death.

His things were next.

Having a house full of guitars, records and comedy videos, books, and other music equipment was hard and becoming harder to attend to, work around and live around. Every room I entered had a guitar, a guitar strap, or a tin full of plectrums. Something to do with his work or blues magazines.

It was tough trying not to cry each time I saw anything. A hat, a baseball cap or anything that was just not me. I was trying to make a new life and didn't want to do much else to these things as they were, I thought, memories that his family might find comfort in. But no one was asking to see or have anything, and I was becoming increasingly annoyed with the life I was trying to build and the weight of all these things still in it.

It was nearing the late end of spring, around April 2020, when I started to feel like I wanted to get things moving and looked at myself and my progress and felt these things; his things were holding me back. I simply could not move for his things. I knew this was brewing in me, and I wanted space. This was going to be a hard decision and one I should make soon.

· · · · · • · • · · · ·

The Flood – 12th August 2020

The decision was taken from me when a flood occurred in the house. The rains were torrential, and I cried and ran as fast as possible to get Morrisons bags, the big ones, and large pots and pans to catch the water flowing like a tap through the ceiling in the front room. The carpet was soaked, and guitars, records and books on bookcases were all at risk. Sofas, TVs, the works. But these were mainly Dave's things.

The insurance man came, and the 'fixer' neighbour took care of everything that needed fixing. All were removed for storage by the insurance company.

·····•·•····

A year later, the insurance company asked me if I wanted these things back, and I said no, except for a white under-desk drawer from IKEA and his guitars; the rest could stay in storage.

They were brought down. But had a lot of organising to do, and again, the fixer-upper-neighbour arranged a local storage unit for me. I had a new front room, and his things were safe.

I sold many of the guitars at auction and still have some left, but I was given the chance of a new home. I remember saying,

"OK, Dave, this was pending, and yes, I've been sat on this for a while. "So, was this your doing?"

He didn't answer,

but I walked past him in the picture on the piano and gave him *'that look'*.

Chapter Nine

The Grief Bank

1 **9th January 2019**

None of us like banking. The traipsing in and out during our lunch hours, the calls, the statements and the charges. But we have to use them, right? We're used to having money stored, and spending occurs, and this is all fine and dandy until we are in the predicament of grief. Now there are two areas I'll share: the practical elements of banking and the hopeful lifestyle banking we will be in, in something called **The Grief Bank**.

········

Let's start with the practical. He's dead. And now you have to do shitty things that make your brain freeze over that were simple once, but now every flippin thing that doesn't work makes you cry. Like a call to the bank and hearing, you have to *do* something you didn't know before, like how to take charge of a shared bank account and bring in a death certificate. That feels awful. The having to explain you are now widowed. But still, feel married (because you are), and each time you say 'widowed', you affirm he is gone. And you cry and explain, and they listen, and they have a bereavement team to help with talking about mortgage payments or whatever you have to deal with. But these calls sometimes have a sorry, we can't do that or this or something else, and there will be a moment where they say,

"Yes, just pop into the bank with blah, blah and some blah, paperwork",

and that sounds simple as. But it isn't because the paperwork has his *name* on it and your name *together*. Or, even separately, and either way, it's still *his printed name*, and this makes you cry. And you remember everything about the day you were in the bank with him.

Back when he was sick because you had to get a joint account ready for when he died so you could pay for the funeral with his money (which would then be yours) because you have none, or very little, or you don't work, or stopped work because he was sick. And you don't want to do this, but you must, and all you imagine you are going to do is buy a coffin and lie on a sofa, and these memories stay and then you are crying, eating ice cream again **in your fuck-sake dressing gown** and the bank has closed.

So this continues into the next day, as the paperwork is also on the kitchen table underneath the funeral director's paperwork and a card you read from a friend you didn't even put up. Still, you read the nice bubble writing and bubble heart above the letter 'i' in Katie or Jackie, and that keeps your attention. You think,

"Ah, she had another kid that I can't recall, and how do I put a silver shilling in the baby's hand in the black cloud I'm in. Ah, well, she'll know I care."

The picture on the front is nice and has a flower on it that you like the purple colour of. You need to look at this colour for some time, and you are distracted with the nice colour and the cross or serenity of the scene and the God that didn't help, and then you are flipping it open again to read that lovely bubble writing like you did in school when you were fourteen and kinda happy.

And 'The Happy' comes and slaps you in the face and says, "Watch how I can get away from you!"

Then you're in a schoolyard playing tag with The Happy and its dexterousness, as he can slip into places and hide like a skinny little fucker, and you are taken with him, and he is funny, and you are sad, but allow him to be in and out of your moment with your teenage years.

Then all this is recalled in the present you are in, with **the bank and the letters and the purple colour** and the paperwork is still underneath something like these cards, or the bus ticket showing two fares into town, the last trip going out without a car. And you now need to put **this little piece of paperwork into a tin** of things that *are* important. And it's not important,

"But it is, it is, it fucking just is!"

And you tie your fuck-sake dressing gown, lie back down on the sofa with the card and the bus ticket, cry big tears because this little thing caused *the big ones*, and you wake up on the sofa at 4am, and the bank is closed.

This will likely go on for some time. Every time, paperwork is called for or asked to be brought somewhere. And you just can't sort shit out, but you need to, and maybe that includes a life insurance policy or a widow's pension that you are now entitled to, that someone helped you find. And the red bill for the gas just landed on the mat and needs paying, and **you like the red writing but can't read the words.**

And you remember in your life before, that red means *'important action needed'* but you just want to leave that and go online to Amazon and buy nice coloured things like candles and reiki cushions or baggy loose clothing or essential oils that aren't red. And then you worry about not having enough money to live on. And you get caught up in words in your head that say,

"live on" and '

"live on", and live on is

"just *so* fucking hard, without them,"

and you look at their picture and tell them so, but they tell you to

"Get the (flip's sake) paperwork!"

And you're shocked out of that idea, and at their not very empathic response, and you struggle through what they tell you to do and say,

"Yeah, yeah, I will!" As you lie back down on the sofa

because the bed really is too fucking big without them, and

"It's not fair that they died, it's just so not fucking fair!"

And they sit and watch you, coax you, touch your head when you're crying, or your arm, or move past you in the shadow of your, fuck-sake dressing gown, near candles that nearly set you alight, in low-lit front rooms where no fire burns because *you* can't chop logs, and the grief and the pain and him chopping logs and the tears. And you just want to stay alight and get to where you can just perform .....**the act of paying bills.**

Oh My God...........................take a self-care break -..........
...... that was hard.

· · · • • · · · ·

The Grief Bank

We need to function. In an economy that now has one less worker in him, does it need to take the worker in you too? No, it doesn't. And this is where you have to, for the sake of you. And yeah, some of their memory, too. They want you to thrive, and you must, for that and them and you. And so, to get to this place, we must find clothes for work.

We have to get washed every day, do our hair, maybe chuck a little make-up on and work the hell out of this place and into the Begin Again life, but to do so, we all have to visit The Grief Bank.

···•·•····

We have to take out a new card. We don't know much about it yet, but within the 14-day cooling-off period (that doesn't really come in 14 days), we have to take out this 'new card' and start 'spending' and have to occasionally call the Grief Call Centre. I'll explain.

Many of us will understand when shopping and paying bills that we may need to ring a call centre to discuss something that isn't quite right or had messed us up at the bank.

If we call these places, if we rely on credit cards, are shopping online and trying to sort out a good deal, we can take out hire purchase and are sometimes only sure what the terms are once we have to make a claim.

We'll be told what the low down is; when we're left on hold, and someone reminds us that we ought to be prepared to pay off a debt or the interest or something we weren't expecting, it feels annoying and downright unfair.

·······••••••···

Grief is the same. We hold a 'grief credit card' when we didn't even know we'd signed an agreement.

We make 'deposits' of tears into this, and on the nights when we've stored plenty and think we're in the red, for days that are too much to bear, we can draw on these for the comfort and quiet, the peace that we need on any rainy day when going out may not even happen. Where we watch windows catch tears from heaven, and they cry for us. But NO.

With Grief Credit and Debt, we're told by the Grief Call Centre,

"This is the price you pay for loving someone that much."

We're put on hold with a

"Press 1 for shit, 2 for pain, and 3 for your grief balance."

To find out how long this shite is going on for. On the numerous days we call in, this takes as long as those calls take to check, hoping there's a change or some change and that we can take out a Begin Again credit for the life we want to still have.

When things get tough, we deposit more tears on the run-up to special occasions. Birthdays, anniversaries, weddings, or deaths, and for Mother's Day, Father's Day, Valentine's, and is there a Wife and Husband Day? We think we'll be in 'credit' by the time we get to family holidays, kids' or grandkids' school plays, daughters giving birth, sickness, and our own or our families' achievements.

The big celebrations that we can barely attend, and all the times when **we cry,** *they should have been here* with us. Right the way through a fourteen-day family holiday, where we take ourselves to bed and look at photos on mobile phones that show they are not there, should be there and was there in spirit.

If we spend wisely in the Grief Bank, we have just about enough to get through our first, second and third Christmas and see that we now take that card out less and less as we become accustomed to the self-applied austerity measure we are now living in. Some of these tears are happy ones, and that's on a separate card. Begin Again, card. We look at the debts on one and see that we're paying them off and are almost done with using it and want to clear the remaining balance with a transfer from Begin Again with a small amount that can be spent once a month.

On those days when it wasn't raining tears on windows and when a friend, neighbour's kid or grandkid smiled their right-through-your-heart smiles.

Notwithstanding, you may find the spending on your other credit cards is going the fuck up! To soothe away the pain, maybe. And this must be handed like bingo online. Only play the two-pence games because **you're gambling with Begin Again credit and sad as fuck debt.** Yes, for holidays, yes, for comfort. But spend just as wisely as you did when you were married. You didn't buy takeaways every night, now, did you?

I decided to make do with a few Aldi or Morrisons frozen meals until I could cook again. Stay in credit everywhere until you have paid this card off.

Chapter Ten

The First Christmas, and more

The first Christmas 2017, we arranged for my grandson to come and stay with me for a few days after the funeral, and I was glad of this. He packed his rucksack and made himself comfortable in the Reiki room.

We still had the kids' bunk beds up. We sat and watched Netflix and played PlayStation games until I became more aware of how boring this must be for him and arranged for us to go to Gloucester Rugby Club. He was a young rugby player, and this might cheer him up and get out from under the grieving widow grandma he was now residing with.

There was lots of work at hand trying to arrange; letters, birth certificates, and proof of who I was to claim a widow's lump sum pension my husband had with his work. So, on our way to dealing with this, we visited the Gloucester Rugby club. They were brilliant, and after explaining to them earlier on a phone call just how important his step-grandad was to him, they presented my surprised young grandson with a warm welcome. There were also some goodies, including a Christmas card signed by the players and a poster.

These journeys were made on buses, and I was glad of the company. Most trips would have been on my own, so it was nice to have had someone with me, and this, too, stopped me from crying.

·· • • •• • •· ·

Around 23rd December, I decided enough was enough, and I should try to put on a Christmas for him and have decorations, a tree or something. But I just couldn't manage it. So, we decided not to stay in the house, travel back to London, and spend Christmas with my brother and daughter.

There was a flurry of activity buying presents for everyone. Making sure gifts would arrive quickly from Amazon. Wrap them at speed, put them into a suitcase and make our way on the last coach from Tewkesbury to London.

·· • • •• • •· ·

We arrived at my brothers' who was hurriedly making preparations for a Christmas Eve party for family and invited family members of my daughter's new partner. Having assured me all would be OK and I would have space and could come in and out of the bedroom if I needed to. It was nice being around people. It was nice being in a home with Christmas and memories and cooking smells, but If I was alone, I would have wanted to stay back at my own house just to be 'with Dave' and probably just a tray of six pigs in blankets rolling around an empty plate. I'm glad I didn't.

I was shocked when my brother asked me to sing on the YouTube Karaoke he had arranged. My husband's funeral was in two days, and I was a million miles away from wanting to hold any microphone or the need to be singing to anyone.

Still, I complied and thought this was good for me and his effort at pulling me through into Christmases we'd shared before. Everyone loved the entertainment, singing Aretha Franklin's songs from I don't know where within me.

It was a nice and quiet Christmas, gentle, in fact. I ate good food prepared with love and watched people live whilst I sat on a sofa. I was told my daughter was being proposed to that evening at a restaurant and would join us later. When she told me her good news, I sat quietly aware of the silence and half full of

'The Happy' that showed itself momentarily, to say

"wow",

because he is still, just a sneaky, can't make him stay, slippery little fucker.

I travel back on the coach back to Tewkesbury alone. I need to get back to prepare for my husband's funeral on 27th December, and I lean my head on the window and cry quietly inside. Looking through, into the white mist and fog of the streets of Tewkesbury.

·· • • • • • • ··

Preparing for the funeral

We prepare his acoustic guitar with flowers and his white blues hat. Debbie and Julie are good friends who come to help me like they did when he was sick and always did when I asked. They are singers and help me sing the song I want to sing, 'The First Time Ever I saw your Face,' and to check I won't bottle it, and they are warm and kind, and we are quiet in the ritual of preparing flowers and grasses for the body of his guitar, like laying flowers *on* his body. Sheathed in all that winter will bring in snow from the days before his death. The home is lit with candles and love.

These two angels are by my side. Helping him to return to The Father that I am close to now. It feels like we are monks inside the sounds of Gregorian chants or Buddhist Temples.

Orange and winter colours are all about us in each flicker of a candle. Sounds resonate through each string of his guitar as these flowers are pulled through. The chorus of his body and wind will play in the high ceiling of the front room, and the shadows on the walls are him, and the sounds are his angelic held soul, being lifted from me.

And there will always be angelic sounds in these times, and we will hear them in the stillness, and the open patio doors of our front rooms where cold may enter and love may rise. And these are the echoes of our hearts and the harmonies of our love, and the night is a blanket laid upon us when we fall asleep, and we are still with them in these moments, these

"Goodbye my darling."

moments. These echoes are remembered, and we know we are helping angelic beings who take charge of this soul. This rising of his death, away from this earth, into the breast and comforting arms of The Mother. And The Son and Holy Ghost are waiting too, and they are there with oils and blessings for the dead. The living, they also hold by their full robes, for *they* are on their knees now and need this Holy cloth to touch. To wrap around them, to hide in the skirts of. Because there is no one else to hold them, everything feels like it is supposed to be happening in this way, and tears are shed with prayers for their soul and yours. And you forgive yourself and God, The Mother, and your mother and the Holy ones for your anger and what you thought was their absence, and they forgive you too. They are busy with a soul and still have time for you. They sent these angels, didn't they?

··•·•·•··

The Day - 27th December 2017

I am wearing black, and there is a child in my house; I wasn't expecting. I am upset as I can't be around anyone new, not yet, and not young, He is my daughter's partners' child, and I quickly gather myself and accept this. I retreat to the bedroom where the make-up is, and the cars are not here yet, and someone offers me a bagel.

"I like bagels,"

but

"I don't like bagels,"

then

"I do like bagels,"

then

"I don't,"

and I wonder where the hell my daughter is as I can't put make-up on without her, it seems.

"It's stupid. I know,"

but

"I don't know,"

and it's like the day I got married, waiting for the cars, and she was busy getting done up and making her way to the house from the hotel, and I was panicking then, and it feels like I'm meeting my betrothed and

"I want my make-up to look nice for him"

and

"He'll be here soon."

and

"Is it too early to drink?"

I get taken outside to sort myself out and get a grip, and I do, and I'm back again, and I'm sorry to everyone for this is the day, like the wedding, when *that* was so important too, and

"I want to look nice or some shit..........."I want to look nice or some shit... Some fucking nice make-up that won't run that will last all day .....because he's nearly here, and I think I look like shit. And I don't want to look like shit. Because he is my husband. Red lipstick, he liked that."

I'm in black with the walking stick from the bad leg still, and I have the black woollen shawl with hippie tassels at the bottom that I wear with my leather-look leggings and black DM-style boots. Because that's what I might have worn when we went out with the suede tassel jacket, that rock chick look, but with my hair down, and

"I don't want to look like shit or even rock chick"

but it feels like I'm going on a date with him. Our last date together. I spray the Armani Black Code perfume he bought me after our first date that he always bought me, and it was always too much, but I like perfume, and he liked perfume, and

"He would have said, "wow,"

if I had my hair down. Or more,

"Yeah, you look nice. Now let's go,"

and I would have moaned,

"Hello? Nice? Is that all?

And he would have said something more like,

"Sorry babes, yeah, you look great."

And I would have swung my fat arse into the Shogun or the LandRover, but moaned about the LandRover and said my

"No lets' take the Shogun, it's got heating,"

and he would have said

"OK""

because he wanted me happy. And then he'd have rubbed my driver-passenger leg, all would be forgiven, and we would have gone to the karaoke pub. And I think of the songs and the drive back home and the tea and toast and tired shag, and the tights I couldn't get off, and he'd say,

"Keep 'em on, haha."

And

"I want to *see* him"

and

"I don't,"

and

"I do."

and

" I don't."

Then I see the cars pull up, and

"I do,

and

"I did,

and

"I did...... I *did* see him! And he **is really dead**. He is there, and the lipstick is red, and the bagel has crumbs, and the lipstick is red, and **the body is dead**."

And no one thinks I'm thinking these thoughts, and they help me into the car, and I'm supposed to be with God, but I'm looking at my husbands' feet in oak, and I think of the tights and him rubbing my feet,

and I'm ready for the vicar who said that

"I shouldn't."

"But no, I insist!"

And the song I must sing, and the people that come, and the words that they'll say, and the children, the cold, the snow and the guitar, that is placed by his oaked feet, while I sing in the Abbey where we wed.

"And the lipstick is red"

and I speak my truths to all. And doors slam, and people leave, and I keep speaking my truths about the man that loved all,

"And the lipstick is red."

The snow is white, and I'm like a child with 'The Happy' hiding behind a grey gravestone and the white he wants to throw, and I say,

"Not yet, one day soon,"

And the snow I took the pictures of, and it's now a Hollywood scene.

"And the lipstick is red."

And the cold on my feet and the barefoot walk needs, like crunching on white hot coals, these pains in the soles of me, that

"I have to resist, **I have to resist**"

And he will be his ash, in the smoke soon and

"I want to smoke"

Then I'm sitting in a car and want to know if the lipstick is still **red.**

· · • • • • · · ·

The Second Christmas - 26th December 2019

I can't remember. I can't remember when he died now;
"What year was it again?"
And I check the calendar on the iPhone for the funeral date
to remind me of when he died.
"How many years? Only two? It feels like more."
I can't recall the children and the presents, or the food and
the music, if there was any singing and what dress I wore and
"If it was blue velvet like I had when he was alive."
I can't recall the make-up or the jewellery, the popping
corks, the TV and the overeating, undereating, smoking ciga-
rettes or burning logs. But I can recall the day after Christmas.
It came and went, and I cried three times, a trilogy of tears;
one in a bed, another just standing and the last on a bus back
home.

It was misty in the high street, half-lit, and no one passing,
even cars, had gone to bed. Families were imagined, wrapped
up in presents and each other behind closed and joyful doors.
Christmas day was over! I'm in mourning, still. A black-veiled
nylon shroud of my every day, not seen, either passed or
through, as if my head is bowed and scarfed. My grief is
catholic and like cataracts behind a waterfall of black. I squint
to puppeteer a half smile for a neighbour on the gravel drive,
more for her than me and put my key in the lock.

·· • • •• • •• ··

27th December 2019

I need to write - it comes as if breaths, slow, repeated waves, like a warm beach that turns into a raucous wave crashing back and forth until a tide draws it out. I am clifftop and howl louder at the storm winds. They let me sing ...and it comes.

Imagined I am stood, arms crucifix stretched to Christ, wearing muslin, wet cloth, wet against skin. Hair whipping against cheeks and wind lapping at feet. The pain drips rapid, like blood, letting. All is coming out.

In Your name, I shout
"take this pain for it is my body
take these tears for these are blood
like life taken by You
I am Banshee
You are the reason I howl
I am in communion with You
are You with me?
Listening? Waiting?
share of *my* body & blood."

Chapter Eleven

Leaving Me, Again? – and You're Not Getting Any

12th May 2018- 5 months in, and it's starting.

"Yes, I'm on my monthly, so fucking what?"

(he's silent)

"You what?"

(he's just staring)

"No, it's my turn to talk. So, you listening?"

(He looks shocked)

Well, good. I got some things to say.

"What fucking right have you got to get involved now in my one day, one flippin day, of being decisive of wanting to take action and not be in this fucking tomb of shite?"

I'm sitting in a front room full of boxes for the loft and charity shop. Gently taking great care of everything you ever, we ever owned and selecting what should be kept or given away.

"No, not even all your own stuff."

Our stuff, clutter and memories all entangled together, dusty, silly, fun, and sad. The big plastic boxes overshadowing and overfull in contrast to the half-empty cardboard ones, post it noted for 'loft' or 'charity shop'. I hadn't even touched *his* stuff yet, just ours. I'm shattered after mending what seems like fragile bones in my hips, knees and leg. A paramedic came to look at that leg that didn't move one morning, in pain and non-weight bearing, saying he was

"Checking in case I'd had a stroke. So, your death is gonna kill us both? No, it ain't Dave. No way."

The GP says something about TIA or Transient Ischaemic Attack, and she's checking on these things too.

"So no, I'm not fucking happy right now, Dave."

Not with me, my body, my room to room, bed and sofa, toilet and kitchen, noodles, toast and sofa life. The sorting, the crying, the fucking sorting and crying.

"No, I'm not happy, Dave."

He's stopped listening, in the look on his face. I'm going for it now.

"I've been so grateful for your help, yeah? That's right? And then you come along and tell me *you're* **releasing** *me*? 'You're' releasing *me*? All gentle and caring and watching me sob my fucking heart out, begging you not to. Just flippin begging you and begging you. Why? No, no, no, babes, please don't. I need you!"

I was distraught, the biggest panic so far. The 'lose you again' panic, but I got through that and had a friend tell me,

"I's OK, he's got things to do. You'll always be married, don't worry. Joined in body, mind and spirit."

So, I calm down. He looks up at me from the sofa, wondering if he's got a chance to speak, then back down again as he can see I'm just drawing more breath. Yes, I'm standing up doing my soap box woman thing. It's not an argument as such. He's not said anything yet, but it's my 'love the sound of your own voice, as he used to say, podium pouring. They can get worse than this if there's a feminist angle thrown in.

"How fucking dare you think that"

Some kind of slighted misconstrued shit I got the wrong end of the stick of yet again and would run with. In these moments, he'd pour another red wine, and I'd simmer to a tepid boil. One where he could still stroke my leg once I'd lay back on that sofa with him.

"Yes, I'm sorry", I'd say.

Eating two, three, or more of the chocolate squares in a hurried, uncontrolled manner. Realising as they melted around my mouth, I was, in fact, due on.

"No, babes, I *am* sorry, I think I'm due a period. I just saw how I was eating the chocolate. I'm sorry."

"All I was trying to say was...," he would offer,

As his opening to most replies, when I was like that then, and I'm like that now. The anger has passed. The man I was chatting to on Facebook Messenger made me laugh, but the noise in the kitchen stopped me laughing. I went to investigate. I see the baking tray on the floor, put it on top of the stove, and clang it to replicate the sound. It fits. I start to walk back to say to the man,

"I can't have a chat any more. I can't have fun in this chat because Dave doesn't want me to."

The last time the man made me laugh, I heard another noise one night in the Facebook Messenger chat. This time the phone in the bedroom, bleeping. Other times the Bluetooth speaker just talking in that way:

"Bluetooth pairing"

at, yet again, more inopportune moments. The moments when I'm ready to practise talking to men again. The acute solitariness being unbearable. I'd end each time with a report to Dave.

"OK, Dave, I understand. So I'll stop, OK?"

Feeling sadness and comforted-ness from my hubby, my dead and caring and loving and needs me, hubby. That confuses the fuck out of me. That is struggling, watching me, hurt by all this, yet wanting this for me too. We're both just as hurt and lonely as the other.

In his **'release-me'** message, he wants me to find a new partner.

"Why?" I sobbed

"Because you're not doing well on your own."

"Yes, I can! I Can! **You're *with* me.** You're helping me. Please don't leave me, babes."

I begged him. Feeling every ounce of abandonment, I feared and lied **I would *not* feel** before he died. I actually told him,

"Don't worry, I won't feel abandoned, like a child, I'll be an adult woman grieving."

So, this is what grief is too? Abandonment? Yes, and he came to tell me that that is precisely what *he* now has to do because **I'm not releasing him**. I was punched in the gut, ripped out all my insides, and strewn across the floor like dirty grey bra straps entangled with knotted black ripped tights he loved me to wear. The stuff you'd not let anyone see.

"These tights are for indoors only, hun."

I'd say, with a wink. He'd smile back. It was all we could do to find a pair that didn't strangle the hell out of me for any duration. We'd both look excited in Primark or Matalan if we found a pair that was extra large, and we'd throw boxes of them in the trolley. I'd lie on the sofa with the tights on, and he would rub my leg, my bad leg, my bad knee, my bad foot and then my arse.

So, I said to the man, that makes me laugh.

"I can't laugh now, I can't, I'm not allowed."

The flirty laughing, the silly laughing, the laugh I did with Dave. I can't, I can't, I can't. I leave a message to tell him so. Then the anger, of all told, rises in me, and I can't even look at Dave's picture. And then my podium out till it ebbs away, and I'm dragged back into the warm memories I have of hubby and me. Me in tights, legs and sofas, his hands and my arse and our love, and I feel trapped.

·· • • • • • • • ··

28th May 2018

I'm adding up the weeks to see how long I'm at now.

"Oh, the five-month mark still?"

But is it? It's about another two weeks as well, so that's a grief gestation of twenty-six weeks. A big sack of grief being born daily, now crowning me on the nightly death-and-birthing bed and bedroom re-runs. This has to be one baby shower of shit. No one is checking if it's twins. I have no iron or vitamins, and fuck me, a clearly absent father.

People watch me carry around this weight, with my shopping bags returning from Morrisons, hiding Jack Daniels under bread noodles, salad and milk. Eyeing me up with this heavy stomach of grief, watching me smoke cigarettes outside and walking past quickly in disdain.

I am a sorry mess, the zombie dead looking like I'm forcibly unwed with this God-forsaken, Jesus Wept and Mary Left, Grief Child inside. This all happens with the return of menstrual blood. Yes, the strange return of my monthly periods after not bleeding for over a year, and I am of the opinion that

"I am definitely for-fuck-sake pregnant."

So, this is some kind of ethereal conception? Well, Mary might have had some scorn over the years from non-believers, but at least she bore the Son of God. I just have some party too hard, son of a low-down Mr Death, that took me behind a pub on a pissy street.

The bleeding womb, housing three squatting spaced out old fibroids, and the belly of Grief Child are investigated, and I'm soon in a hospital overnight having a procedure and feel very much alone.

All is well, and I don't carry a litter that includes cancer, and I'm travelling alone back home again and into a bed with a reiki cushion and some essential oil making a mess on the side.

· · • • • • • · ·

I lay on my side and missed him being there in person. I tell him anyways about the results.

"So yeah, it's not likely to be cancer, they said."

He's a bit silent.

"Yeah, I, um, think it's probably not too. So er?"

I'm waiting for some kind of reply, and he's flippin not listening!

"What the actual fuck? This is bloody important, and you're not listening? Or answering?"

Actually, more that he was simply not answering. I get pissed and try to storm off to the kitchen, but it's a slow stomp because the

"Light bleed that might occur and you'll be a wee bit un-comfortable for a few hours,"

turns out to be seriously fucking painful. When I had active Bleed for England fibroids, he would get me my tablets and painkillers or rub something, my foot, my leg, my back, while I moaned and groaned on a sofa till the stop the blood tablets kicked in. So yeah, I was expecting all that.

"I'm his wife, for fucks sake!"

But now nothing.

"You're a fucking little liar, David. Really? With your 'Just call me anytime you want a hug when it gets so bad at night and "blah, blah blah, not fucking listening now to you darling!' No, you're a fucking liar. I've been out there all on my own and come back, and you got the *cheek* to not even check in on me. Or even listen to my update. My, I got this update. You're indoors and still lying around while I gotta do all this fuck-sake cleaning?"

Nothing, just a slow, unconfident, but resolute flick of his imagined Heaven Highlights Newspaper.

"Well fuck you!" I shout

and then sling dishes in the sink under hot running water. I'm mumbling under my breath and expect him to come into the kitchen when I finish the plates and definitely by the time I get to the saucepan with porridge burned on.

He still hasn't come. And I remove the apron over my breasts and think,

"Well, yes and fuck you! You're not getting any of *this* when I get to bed."

Chapter Twelve

Did You Hear The One About The Widow? - and Costa-Del-Shite

"Ha, can you get even *more* quiet in a widow's day?" Yeah. And

"How many widow jokes can I make about quiet times or just being a widow? Did you hear the one about the widow at the barbecue?"

Or

"Have you ever seen a widow running? Do you ever see a group of widows on a works do? Is there a widows' disco anywhere? Do we all wear grief briefs?"

There are no punchlines to any of these other than the one in the gut. But sometimes, very rarely with those that know, we widows can laugh. Yes, together, we can have a pull it-from-our-boots and bawl with dark humour. The sort that makes others with live husbands say

"Ouch, and fuck sake, that's so heavy. Can we laugh at what she just said? Is it acceptable?"

And the way we see those of you, 'the normals', who are trying your best to at least communicate and not cross the road. The

"Hey, how are you doing now?"

Or "You'll get there."

And worst of all, - Time is a healer."

Our keep-to-ourselves replies are - "Now?"

and - "I'll get where? Up to Heaven with him?"

Or lastly, -

"Yeah, time is a healer, and I hope in time, you'll get over the imagined headlock punch I'm giving you"

and your

"Shut-the-fuck-up stupid mouth"

back into their reassess mode, internally screaming,

"He's still fucking dead!"

·········

It is so incredulous the levels of anger some of us feel. The coping and niceties we have to muscle up to say something that isn't so down your fucking throat. The bucket of black hot oil we're hosing you down with now, and I am to **'stay in the land of the living'**. These want to be helpful but can't bring them back; nice as fuck living.

So yeah, we crazy dark-humoured widows laugh at how we get by. The ***keep it in*** and furiously seek the

"Say something that sounds normal' replies.

The one-liners that betray our dead-real, death deal.

"Oh, you know, mustn't grumble."

Or simply sighing in a not too bassy, achy heart ripped-out tone. A more melodious seaside wind chime noise that says

"Oooh, we got some sunshine today, huh?'

and back of the head wave as we walk off, lip quivering. Or the worst of all and in all truth the

"Yeah, I *am* getting there. I went to the garage to get milk today."

To be met with a blank nervous stare as that just sounds like I'm proud of my 'lady going mad' talk.

We own mouths or thoughts that are vicious and uncontrolled, like proud short drug dealers with rottweilers or bull mastiffs raging leash-pulling grief dogs that we let loose in a busy shopping centre or other social settings of more than one.

When we're on buses or trains or on phone calls with cold callers selling insurance. And especially with those that address letters to dear Mr _____ house owner, Our records show that you are entitled to..blah blah blah offer. And *my* return offer is that you are entitled to hear that

"He is still fucking dead, I own the house, update your piss-poor records and don't call me back!"

Laughter is yet another tool I use to deal with or escape from grief. In poetry mode, I am one step closer to a cathartic outing, poetically made. Some are not bad, most not so good, all rhyming and just plain letting. Little crafting, some great, it-just-happened poems that did work but a soothing lexicon elixir taken daily, in the main. A salve that inked its way out of me, in black font, and blacker nights. Away from the too-sunny, stay indoors, hidden from those designed-to-make-you-happy days.

·· • • • • • • • ··

Costa Del Shite - 28th May 2018

I make my way to the shops, wet-wiping face, pits and never again but hopeful regions, hiding away behind my big sunglasses. I need bread, milk and chocolate and to see human beings. I might hang with some human beings later today, but the bread, milk, and peanut butter toast I'm gonna have will boost me with the minimally afforded calories I need to get showered before I do. Someone has asked me to go out. I'm such a grief fraud. Showing all kinds of Facebook posts about me being smiley-icon happy, up for a night out, day out. Any takers? When all I wanna do is stay in the Netflix, Now TV, and YouTube arcade I've made indoors. There are no real people here that can help salve the laugh-less days unless I reach out for the phone.

"Hey, (widow number one), how you doing today?"

Soon meaning 'guess how I'm doing today.'

"Just wanted to touch base and see how you are."

Also meaning, I know you've likely just wet-wiped and peanut buttered your way out of the better half of 10am. Widow number one tells me hopeful half-truths as we try to cotton-wool each other through the next twenty minutes of support. We know we will both hang up and cry some semi-big tears in both relief and

"Shit, so I'm still here," rhetoric.

Yes, support and protection. I am fierce about and angry as fuck about their pain too. The

"Why'd you have to do this to her too? You bastard"

but don't know who I'm swearing at. God? The Universe? That bitch called life? Or the bastarding brain tumour entity masquerading as one single illness in each of our loved ones.

It is not one single entity. It is a Facebook-Esque growth permeating all across the globe, in our little homes and our now, probably less than, life-limited lives and our loved ones' now smaller, debulked brains. Spreading and putting little BT (brain tumour) blobs all over the fucking world. Tentacles of non-halting, breeding, wired up and blood pumping connection. Now, connecting us in pain,

"You utter fucking networked cunt."

Yes, the anger is for the Facebook global brain tumour and grief network you leave us with. We're supposed to be happy, grateful for now having to log in to each other for us to cope with 'that hour' that 'help me' moment or that day. Yes, because Facebook is at least there. It's a slap in the face; chuck us a welcome line on your BT departure, their departure.

"Would all passengers boarding the trans-global BT 101, departing from gate Life-As-You-Knew It? Please make your way to gate GRIEF H E L L for one last spit back at the fires below. Please be advised no friends over 100 ml of pure joy will be allowed to accompany you, and be prepared to leave them at Passport Dressing Gown Control."

So, we get aboard the flight of Make A Life Again and speak to each other.

"Oh no, I've never been here before. Yes, I'm sure it's gonna be one to remember. Nervous? Yes. I'm already drinking Jack

Daniels. At least we get to have a double allowance in Guilty Free."

We speak and soothe and drink and smile and laugh and get nervous at take off to the Costa Del Shite. There are no kids with us. No inflatables, iPads, nail varnish, lip balms, sparkly tops, perfectly manicured toes. No cheeky extra-large Durex boxes on special offer at Amazon.

"Wow, that's a good deal, babes."

in our carry-ons. No lube or strawberry tasting, ribbed or nobbled or cock-ringed, rubber, sex fun things. No coconut oils to entice. No sexy plunge costume with matching sarong that he'll see slip and show a browning thigh that he can't resist touching. Right there,

"Right *there* in front of a cocktail waiter?"

The

"Sorry babes, I couldn't help myself"

Laughs...as you playfully give flashing scorn eyes over sun-glassed eyes he loves to wink back at. No suntan oils to rub and free up sexual touch in the guise of *rubbing it in*. No,

"Let's go for Siesta!"

When you know what that *really* means, before an early dinner and sunset waters edge, wined for earlier nights with more and more and more of each other in bed. Hot and coconutty and strawberried and sweaty and cooled naked with the bedside fan, and sneaky smoking cigarette in almost naked sarong thingy. Out the window, crickets watching, humming along to your own hum of love. The falling bounce back into bed complaining,

"Yaaa, you're still sweaty, lol. "

"Ah, sorry, where's the wet wipes?"

"No, get a shower, hun!"

No quick wee, bum stuck to the seat, making you squeak and laugh as you get up. Making *him* laugh as he thinks you just 'lady farted.' The quick affirmation of

"We-hey and thank you *very* much, that was flipping fab."

Doubly announced as you glance at your sweat-curled hair that he has just semi-permed for you in his extra horny holiday effort.

"Yes, I miss you! Oh, God, I do."

Climaxing in this fuckless hologrammed you.

"What the fuck now?"

Bleeding soul, heart, and pussy aching loss.

Chapter Thirteen

Stay Alight – Poetry and Performing - Butterfly - The Visit

Stay Alight – 28th May 2018

"I gotta stay light. I'm gonna stay alight. A heart that's been darkened in grief. Stay alight, stay alight, get a light, have a smoke, stay alight. Bring it, bring it, bring it to the fore. Get the gravel, get the dust, get the stones, shove them in the grate. But air it and stay light. Stay alight. When your heart says it's time for more and your head says no. Everything you do is about trying.... to ....come.... to ....terms with *something or other*.

It's like a HP account at the end of term of service. The end of this, the end of that. Working out what your final payment is. It's all there. It's all there in the small print of grief. How to overcome, how to pay more, how to stay more, be more, do more, want more, feel more. All of it. It's all there in the small print that nobody... wants.... to ....fucking ....read. But you have to. So, you stay alight. Finding the light, keeping the light. Stay... the.... Fuck... alight. Get a light. Have a smoke. Stay alight.............

.......Find it and do something with it. When..... When people say, 'oh, you're so good at this, you're so good at that.' It kind of...it bounces in like a, like a, like a tiny match that can't light fully, and it just goes out. You see a teeny glimmer of something, and you know that the wood in the match ain't thick enough, strong enough to keep that light bright. So you just use it to have another smoke. You use it for a glimpse. A tiny movement around the house: to candle.... to toilet.....to back to bed. But you don't use it to live on! We can live on that! That heat, that light, that fuel, we can live on that. We could have a life on that......

I just need a whole...fucking...box!

And I'm feeling it now. I'm trying to keep it alight. Fan the flame. Keep it alight. Get a light. Have a smoke, have a drink, have a smoke, have a drink, have a smoke. Get alight, stay alight. But keep it alight, be the light. Be the light."

··· • • • • ···

Getting out – Writing and Performing Poetry -Food For Thoughts – 9th June 2018

I'm writing poetry, and these words are doing something strange to me now. I feel the need to share this with *the world that doesn't know*. Like people do when they are in love from a mountain top, or at the end of the street, swinging themselves around a lamppost after kissing **them.** The whoever **them,** they are, and you just want to tell the world! But *this* is not like that. The motivation is, the need is, the desire is to

"Tell the world ma!"

But I am *not* on top of the world. I'm in the **underworld,** where dead people drink bourbon against a wet brick wall and a lamp that flickers on a someone-died-there street. The shady dead. The don't go near 'em, dead. They are the hookers and pimps, drug dealers and pickpockets of the underworld dead. They see me coming and laugh, smirk their

"New here?" smirks,

and I move passed them without talking. I enter the underworld in this scene at Café Rene: underground brickwork, an arched cavern with brown wooden chairs that a stripper might use, a bar that is closed with bottles of dead-people bourbon and dark walls all around.

At night it's filled with people dancing, modern reggae tracks and garage, hip hop and grunge music. And I've danced there and had the stumble walk up the stairs to smoke cigarettes on a cobbled alley with wooden beer tables and ashtrays. I stumbled back down and danced on those nights, avoiding toilet paper walk-throughs near toilets and long-haired cool rockers.

But now, in the afternoon, it is dark and silent. I am the first to arrive at the poetry reading. I perform the first of many performances that take me out against my agoraphobic wishes as I am jettisoned into speaking these truths in Gloucester, Worcester, and Cheltenham and join The Gloucestershire Poetry Society at Facebook and write there constantly.

Over the next three years, I post poetry there, and soon, I am published in three anthologies. I post my art pictures with poems. Photos and images that show the visual of the pain I was in, formed new poems, made new friends, and new abilities to keep on writing.

I applied for a writers' commission with an organisation called Paper Nations for marginalised writers. I told them about my book and the one-woman show, This Shite Grief and the inner and outer theatre I had now become as a poet and performance artist. I had been in theatre, and I knew this was something that was the next stage and the ever-evolving newness in me.

I am like a new bloom or some kind of weed you want to pull out, but it still has a little something, so you leave it for a few days. Well, I *was* left for a few days, and along with other poets and writers, won an award as Marginalised Writer for South West England!

I am full of what this now brings me with surrealist poet and Mentor Ronnie McGraff. The workshops and other writing I find in myself. I am doing what I told him I would do.

"Dave! I won the award!! I flippin well won!"

He is on top of the piano in a picture, smiling and quietly says,

"Go on, girl."

A new widow messaged me early in my writing on Facebook, and we typed our hurts there and also spent time on the phone. She saved my number on her phone as 'Tish-Writer and Poet', and I had never thought I would be seen as such, but I was to *her*, and now that she had told me, I promised myself I would say this and feel it and be it.

And now, I *can* call myself a writer! I met people and poets, started to make friends drank in pubs in Gloucester bars and pubs called The Tigers Eye. I sing on microphones whilst drunk, just like I used to do in Tewkesbury with Dave. And I'm right in the middle of my own world, and I am becoming. Something, someone, something other than widow.

Become your becoming. I am becoming. I don't know what yet, but I rise up and take his ash and soar from the ground I was in as if sleeping cosily in his grave, hugging and **loving the bones of him**, and I emerge. I am not a butterfly. I am like a weed, but still acceptable. I am like a moth. A winged and dark moth that is fascinating to watch at a distance. A moth that came from the ground. I am large, fat-bodied, and dark, bottle-green winged, with stories to tell. Old stories of wonder and talking with death and voices of husbands and dark. The shadows of my life fluttering in candle-lit rooms. I am there, and I am formed.

·········

Butterfly – The Visit 29th July 2018

I am aroused at 5.50am in bed to feel a touch between my shoulder blades on bare skin. I wonder if it's me dreaming, and I stay face down on the pillow. It comes back again and I am almost too hopeful and frightened that if I turn around it will be you and you will have disappeared.

I feel sweat and heat begin to form between my chest and the mattress below. It's like a cross between a hot flush, anxiety and fear, and I have to commit to either staying there and falling into a dream or turning around and seeing you leave.

The next touch makes me decide again finally that I am not dreaming. I shoot up in the bed, turn the lamp on, and then tread the carpet to quickly flick on the 'big light.'

I am tired and think I'm seeing things until there is no mistaking it, a butterfly. You are not in the room. I feel despondent until I see small shadows flicker behind the bedside cabinet. I look at your picture in the family frame just above the lamp and realise the stained-glass hanging window art of the Virgin Mary is not there. It's been there for as long as I can remember, and its suction cup never failed ever. But tonight, it seems to have, at the touch of a butterfly.

She had dropped at some point in the night and is now behind the bedside cabinet with the butterfly. It's resting, then fluttering, throwing slim shadows up the wall. I'm hoping it's not a moth, as I can be scared of these as I reach down to retrieve Mary. I can't see properly and move the love heart picture of us at our wedding onto the bed.

I bring Her and you up at the same time. I feel it *is* you and that **you have come to visit**. At this point, I know I want this to be recorded, and I reach for my phone and take pictures.

You fly upward and away from the bedside cabinet. I place the Virgin Mary art firmly back onto the family picture frame. I have a moment of thanks for Her and you all at the same time, and half believe I have it all wrong, and I am merely making associations until shadows of your wings are caught from the corner of my eye of you circling the light above and then fly passed me again.

Hanging on the wall is the framed first-year (paper) anniversary picture I bought for you, a faux newspaper heading with our photo and the headline; 'Dave and Tish Named Britain's Blues Couple of The Year' subheading 'The Camps Celebrate Their 1st Year Anniversary In Love'.

You land on this anniversary headline on the glass and remain there until I fully acknowledge your spiritual presence. I begin to cry soft tears of gratitude. The quiet tears of peace and hearts full of light and prayer. We are together, and you are **telling me you love me, that you come with God, with Mary and that you and Mary are with me.**

Once I've acknowledged you in this way, you move to the top right-hand side of the picture frame surround and perfectly mirror the toy stick-on butterfly our granddaughter placed on the corner of the frame below. Resting there for a while, I stood and just watched you and thanked you through my quiet tears. They roll down each check, and I'm full of a silent inner flutter, not wanting this to stop, **to ask you questions** and just *be* with you wanting to talk again and hear your voice, but I'm caught up in taking photos and **the rapture of this very moment**.

I see you flutter past and land on the headboard, resting and then onto my pillow. You do one lap around my head up into the light above me and then towards the window. This message has been given, and you need to leave.

You are resting on the rolled-down window blind in front of creaky casement windows that haven't been opened since you died. I watch from the other side of the bed and have taken all the pictures and let you out, knowing we are turning a corner.

·· • • • • • • • • · ·

30th July 2018

Over seven months, I've been poet-ing my way through the grief almost daily. I write, and it cannot stop. I am beside myself with wanting to get words out onto paper into the air and away from me. They are of early grief, aching, bartering with God, family struggles and fears of living alone or at all. I have shared them, performed them, spoken, miked up and shared each in pain. I am wholly enamoured with the spoken and written word. I am in love with words!

I've also been testing myself by talking with men. Men, men, men – how the word lands on 'n' and stays a good while if you're happy to be in their company. 'Nnnnnnnnnnnnnn' I say, albeit virtually, it is still lowercase' nnnnnnn.'

Chapter Fourteen

Men - The Janitor, Prayer Man, Would-be-Suitor, Fixer and Player

I am a widow. I was married, and a man I married died. Therefore, I am wid–OWED. Owed a life without him, owed a return to work, a life, to love and play. Can that happen? Can I play? What does play look like without him? Men *can* play a part now. I can direct these attentions in myself and in them - from them into a new me.

·· · · • • • • · · ·

I am 'becoming', a story of the newness in me. A telling of a woman's grief and love and ability, stability, credulity, sexuality in the 'find herself' again. 'Scripts of the Mother' fall into my psyche from the file labelled, 'Irish Catholic Mum.' These are from the back catalogue' Life and Relationships'- circa 1986.

"You're nothing without a man,"

after a break up with my daughter's 'too handy handyman' let's call him, with his too ready to 'land one on me,' hands.

I rebuke this in her and him, find myself out of his abuse and then proceed to flourish, educating my mum and myself that I am *indeed* something, anything and everything without a man, had a fourteen-year lesson in being without a man after many loves with women and learned much, including that there are also handy women with much too handy 'land one on me' hands.

·•••••••·

Back to men and play. They are cast into the roles of Would-be Suitor, Janitor, Fixer, Player or Prayer Man.

I am in the theatre of my becoming. The chrysalis stage of new thought, feeling and action. The metamorphic design and colour of the wings that I will set myself free with. I will stay on sun-soaked leaves, hidden in shade to learn the lines, edit scripts and walk from the shadows.

The direction I take may be filled with fear, and I may get burned by the flames, darting towards lights, up and around and in and out of danger, resting where I can, sugar-sipping cups of the other and strengthened in my own flight, up and away from ashes. Pupae to the phoenix rising into the theatre of a new life.

·········

The Janitor

The 'Janitor' comes to fix lights, not on a stage, but a security light outside my widow's house that I cannot fix. I am stuck in failing widow hands holding 'too heavy' screwdrivers and ladders that reach cobwebs on windy autumn nights. These are the times that widows fix shit. The 'make it more complicated than it needs to be' shit, on wet ladders in slippers and fuck-sake dressing gowns.

I am all a flutter, begging for his sympathy, ability, proximity, and listen to me, empathy. He complies. I've shared my usual story that now falls fully from my mouth without censorship. There is nothing that holds this story back, ever. No social faux pas made, I do not berate myself or syphon this smaller tale out of me, there is no edit, no be succinct, I cannot be, on this edge of madness, this is me, please help me, chitty of a chat.

For all that stop, to hear the woman grief maiden in distress made mad in solitude, tears and a lifetime of unanswered medical whys, there are two options; stay and help or be sorry and leave.

He stayed. Three hours of coffee and kitchen talk on repairs to a house and a plan that would work, on solitude, widowhood, families and loneliness, including his own.

This was humanity, not his MAN-it-y. It was not a pitch or needfulness play at any possible sexual attraction – nothing was noted, realised, allowed or uttered from him to me or me to him. Nothing was at stake. No tension was made. It was an easy acceptance of one another.

Our separateness and pain remained and were nurtured as being the invisible plus ones we brought to sit beside us on two cluttered chairs next to the honey and mustard on a 'can't see the table' gingham tablecloth.

He left me with a number, widow rates and fixed light outside to make me feel safe. We grew business and friendship close in the weeks and months to come. His fixing things on the list and accepting the triggered tears when, 'pass me that' and 'man up a ladder,' reminded me of Dave.

As I grew stronger in myself and DIY, I called him less and less. The last time I noted how it was coming to an end. I allowed myself to feel that this was a sending of a human with humanity. One that helps me, and for me in particular, to be free of dual Scripts of the Mother and the plays of 'handyman-handed' ways. I'll call these the Man-it-y days, helping in ladders and steps and in and on that grief stage.

·· • • • • • • ··

The Fixer

The Fixer or fixers, as there are a few. The first online, was 'Sammich Man', Paul, whom I greatly appreciated in helping me eat again, listened to my poetry and excerpts of my book, an actor from Liverpool who was truly encouraging, and much more. Through Messenger, he listened and supported my ever-inward, ever onward writing, posting my poems on his Facebook' poem of the day' posts, and laughing and joking when I could manage it. He was great and extraordinarily helpful and widow-boosting. His Facebook quick responsive 'atta girl' or comedy gifs or just make me laugh at my feminist outpourings by his favoured gif return:

'Now get back in that kitchen and make me a sammich,'

never failed to make me laugh! His not-overly-soppy warmth and kindness were very encouraging, like, 'come on, girl, don't mess too long in the pit of despair.' That was really what I needed, and yes, writing and having feedback, connection and support like this was very important. I slowly moved on with his help from 'sammiches' to hot dinners and posted pics on Facebook to show him and the world I was doing ok.

·····•·•····

The Prayer Man

'The Prayer Man' was an online connection through poetry and writing. While scrolling through the posts in a Facebook writing group, I saw one that caught my eye. A Buddhist writer and Reiki Master in the early stages of launching his book. It was about domestic abuse that he had experienced and told a tale that resonated with me. Women and men's experiences of abuse. I notice my need to do something, help someone, be distracted from my grief, and offer to help market the book across social media. Working with words again would be good for me. We agree to talk and do so every day. The marketing turns into editing, and I am with him 100%. The calls are daily, and I am glad that my counselling background helps through the edits as they are most painful and shocking.

We are now friends and try to talk about meeting for a coffee once the book is on its way to launch, but I am terribly stuck in the house. I am so awfully unable to plan a journey without crying. The vastness of the skies is too much as my husband resides in the vastness there too. It would be like a journey with him into a wide-open field, and then it suddenly gets dark, and I'm supposed to be running to safety.

Clearly, in these 'widow film' edits, I would have already lost a torch, wore high heels and invariably fallen over in a rain-sodden field, got up and dragged myself to the wrong side of some town they don't like 'strangers' in. And, what stranger thing than a dressed-in-black London widow, traipsing woefully, crying and arguing with her dead husband, in the middle of a country lane? The ask of a couple of villagers leaving a pub, with three more pints than they should have, "help me?" (haha) is really the worst.

We are a scary bunch, us widows. We are the worst in dark country lanes and dark cinemas we sit alone in. Dark doorsteps and doorways we can't move away from. Or our dark widow humour that jokes with darker than me, Mr D.

Death in his dark robes, a Burke and Hare modern lick, like Neo from The Matrix and the moves he made, slick, quick, taking a husband just like that, checkmate!

"Follow the White Rabbit,"

As some Trinity wannabe, I remind myself every time I light a candle. The tragedy of it all is that we widows, in this film set of unreal surrealness, just so want to be in a pub wearing black and to just sit with others, not necessarily talk to them. That's way too much, but just *be* in other's company and not just friends with Mr D, revelling in our blacker skies, grey clouds, neck aching, star watching on doorsteps and his dexterous night moves. Not moving quick like Trinity, just ongoing step by step.

We are able to watch and desire to partake in small amounts of this. To sit like we used to with a husband, across a wet bar table, playing with beer mats, laughing momentarily at overheard jokes with drunk philosophical and harmless regulars and a barman, who smiles and winks at us, enjoying the banter he's having with them. With us looking back at each other and smiling, spilling crisps or peanuts. Me laughing at him trying to eat pork scratchings. Or trying to touch my leg under the table, me asking for one more prosecco when I knew I should have just ordered a pint of cider, but today is my playful 'feel-like-a-lady' day.

(Oh, here we are, the memories and the tears). Mr D and *his* pork scratchings at tables he invites me to sit at seemingly on the regular, with all the family members he's taken from me. We are widows and the bereaved with a new set of you-don't-wanna-have friends, comfortable in dark shadows, dark bras, grey skies and darker thoughts.

·········

Prayer Man and his book are finished, and we part our telephone company and friendship. We have a few calls that highlight more to me about my vulnerabilities as a widow when I ask him for advice about men and learn new things about myself. It seems I am much less able than I ever was to prise out my own self-esteem from the weeds of Widowland to nurture this, make it strong and honour myself and make real the best parts of my enduring want, to not be alone, with the toss a coin into risk with another that ends badly. I cannot set boundaries with what I should be as a woman and widow, being swept off my feet or choosing to be alone. This was the risk I took, the friendship I soon lost, and a price I paid for it landing at the feet of the next.

·········

The Player

A theatrical whirlwind romance, and a gust of wind that takes up all the grief and throws it into a large black bag at the back of the wardrobe. I tried earnestly to scoop it up carefully every time I opened the door for my slippers, but I could see it there waiting for me.

Sometimes it spilt out onto the floor, and I'd have to shut the door on it shoving the boots and trainers back in till I could squeeze it shut once more and then spin off somewhere without the pain. I decided I would take some out when he wasn't watching to put into an invisible rucksack I would secretly carry with me when I was with him.

I tried earnestly to keep this beside me, carefully draped over the back of a chair, behind a kitchen door, and when things got hard, I would touch the ashes on my return home and say sorry.

There were problems that I knew were unhealthy for grief and simply as a person. I knew this was all too fast, and I constantly needed to end this relationship.

I fought myself and the aloneness I felt, weighing up what was right for me, and the final choice came for me to end this during a family crisis and a baby grandson in a hospital with pneumonia.

I had my dead husband by my side. He was the one I could turn to and prayed to.

After this, I also learned more about my co-dependency and avoidance of grief. I am still working out what this period was therapeutically for me. Then I opened the door on my black bag of grief, pulled it out of the wardrobe and sat in the middle of it.

··········

The Would-Be-Suitor

The would-be-suitor a year or so later. There was a time when I thought I was ready for something, but I was not sure what.

The long-haired man, a new friend with coffee and companionship? Finding friendship again. The precursor to finally navigating the complex world of Widow Dating and crashing. I learned how to read the stars, passing life buoys and headlands into ships and my own wreckage on a few wrecked souls or would-be-suitors. Nothing that I would be ashamed of, but I was definitely not ready for anything again. And finally...

··········

Fixer Number Two - The Builder

The Builder, a neighbour, called Dave and his wife, Sam. Dave, who fixed my house after the flood (of tears), the actual August flood in my widow's house. The carpeted front room floor was completely soaked, ripped up, and wet blinds and rubbish that was all disposed of. He and his team did the repairs to everywhere that was needed. Painting and new flooring, new wall lights and trips to the attic and outside and up and down ladders with bags of wet roof insulation and cups of tea and helping lift and carry and finding me new local storage units for the stuff I still wanted but didn't want back inside.

I was so grateful to him and Sam. They even gave me gifts of two lovely rugs, a TV that no one wanted that was put on the wall, and more 'come join us' drinks in their garden. Their kindness and skills brought me a new widow-getting-better home. I was in a new front room with light and sunshine streaming through, and lastly, his advice to put myself and my life first, to 'get back out there' to 'smile' and 'come on and join in.' Come and be with them at their distanced garden parties on summer nights with a bottle or two shared with neighbours on our side.

Three homes of neighbours to the right that all met at Dave and Sam's Garden Bar. We even had a karaoke night, with the PA perched on the patio doorstep, iPhone playlists and a microphone, and it felt like we were out at a pub, and all of us laughed. Until I started crying, and three neighbours brought me back in. I cried the big drunk widow tears

"Yeah, but he's de..he...heaad," sniff, belch, hiccup.

·········

I saw all these people as fixers, movers and shakers. Shake-me shakers, saying,

"Come back to this world, Tish. We are here, and it's alright, and you can live in it too!"

And they'd all give the nod and a wink when I spoke about getting out for a coffee with a man because they wanted me to live! They all wanted me to live!

And they listened to me talk on doorsteps or coped with my smudging the house with sage and other lovely smelly stuff wafting along garden bushes, with Native American music drumming loudly, in my reiki baggies, or me singing flippin loud rock songs or playing my reiki, or rock choir songs again and again, or playing the piano on the white keys only through the darker days, and would hear all these things through the open or closed patio doors and, no one thought I was mad, and their smiles were a balm, and their care was plentiful.

Chapter Fifteen

Poetry - My New Love

Now back to poetic advances. I can now fully cry, eat, not eat, wash, not wash, cry some more, fluff cushions, and play with a screwdriver in some pseudo-maintenance fashion on something small that was perfectly fine, but I score up for 'achievement for the week'. I digress; poetic ways of being are here to stay.

I am happy to have joined a Poetry Society. I am in love with poems and words and my dead husband.

Love is a drug, and we are addicted to its power in the moons we look at, the sunsets and sunrises, attributing these to our very own version of love and stereotypes that fit.

Love is chocolate, is cake, is ice cream, is the sugar hit that satisfies when we're watching that great movie with a husband by our sides, on sofas with popcorn and foot rubs, bum rubs, and the last of the pizza dipped in garlic mayonnaise.

·· • • · • • • ·

LOVE IS CARBOHYDRATES!

We are satisfied, stay still and not exercise and rush to these couch potato days after work, because we said public vows to him and secret ones to a sofa. We are surfing waves in seas of blue, in tides of curly fries, sandwiches and sex, hummus and olives, and tv remotes are our sextons to deserted islands and beaches in the ebb and flow of our TV soap operas. In marriages where there are sofas in houses, this is what happens. It is comfortable. We are not wise of what is to come, that we may become, widow-wise. We are unaware that we, too, will be caught in a wide widow's net in the nightly dangerous dark waters, in the shoal of tears. Widows, like black salmon, on the River Styx, swimming against the move-on. We move through stages and currents of healthy grief psychology to the place where we met. On rivers edge, spawning wedding re-runs and our eggs, captured nightly in our oaths and offerings of prayers and tears, despising Death in this, to a husband that is now becoming our dead 'God.'

·· • • · • • • ·

POETRY IS PROTEIN!

It is the lean meat we should be eating. It strengthens us daily. We search for, build up with, and make protein bars and cakes from. Poetry is the gentle 'get through this' whisper, bubbling in the chicken noodle soup we cook, or the loud and angry venison villanelle that demands self-grilling with a side of blackcurrant sauce. Poetry is eggs and milk and cottage cheese, with balsamic vinegar tears. It is the sustenance that counteracts crying carbs on hips and hearts. It is touching carpaccio in its raw state, dressed in our 'keep on living' oils and bleeds onto pages and plates in the rare and medium steaks we scribing widows are. We strengthen up on words, eat this, be this, become strong. Without this, we are all the foods we should not eat.

········

I am writing. It began very quickly, as I said in the beginning, did I say, well here it is. I am writing to exorcise and exercise, weight lifting words above my head, above my weight and footstep around a ring, shadow boxing with myself, with *Grief: The Kickboxer* that will fuck you up, sister. She is dexterous, can outsmart your every move, the ones you make from widow beds to windows, to front doors and beyond.

She will claw at you, sideswipe, is the uppercut again and again in a quivering jaw. Bitch, she will knock you out and kick you while you're down. She will jump out of rings and meet you on buses and trains, trip you up in the store, at checkouts, whilst ringing through your yoghurt and noodles, and land one on you when you least expect, Pink Panther Cato, wearing black. Wrestle you to the ground in car parks, in churches, while taking a rest on park benches, waiting for you in rounds three and four, and behind your own front door. Grief is a kickboxing ninja.

·····•••···

Poetry – Love - Loss and Grief

Poetry has been the most significant connection to an emotion I have ever experienced. From age six, my older sister sat and read poems to me after brushing my hair. This, I recall, was on a Sunday night when everything was peaceful, and the family were getting prepared for school the following day. It was soon after my mother left my father and us seven children in his care. This was when my sister was twelve, a special memory for me. It was the most comforting thing I could have experienced at that time of significant loss to us all. When she died in 1986, I didn't write poetry for her. She attended Hillcroft Women's College in Surbiton as part of a City Lit study retreat in creative writing. I asked the Universe whilst meditating one day,

"What do I need to do to be a writer?"

and in the images I was given and strange 'coincidences' that occured with an A4 programme being sent to me in my Harrow home, was **spiritually led** to the college and to a **VHS video.** (This and other family spiritual happenings, is a whole other story) It was of *her* performing poetry!! And of other women poets and was about to be archived. I cried my eyes out whilst watching her perform, took the video (please forgive me) and shared it with my family. This was the only live footage anyone had of her and I showed the video to her eighteen-year-old son, saying,

"This was your mother. She was amazing, and you should be very proud."

I have written about her in a poem called Nubian Queen and a book (now misplaced) of the same name.

· · · • · • · · · ·

As a teenager, I retreated into poetry. It was my go-to place, along with the diary I'd written daily that held many teenage secrets. I'd grown from listening to poetry to writing it and stayed heavily in the end rhyme. At around fourteen, possibly fifteen, I had been punk, if you can call backcombing your hair and wearing leopard skin tops, anarchic punk!

So, listening to music that the pissed-at-society youth were listening to and the early music of The Jam, Kate bush, Blondie, and others became my way of accessing fantastic imagery in the poetic and political of my own and the UK's social history within those lyrics, those words.

At fifteen, I was exposed to Plato and read poetry once more.

Demetrius was a beautiful Greek student that hung around Toynbee Hall in Whitechapel. I mixed with overseas students in a local bar, and he took me on a date; Hyde Park, summer, me sitting against a tree, eating Boursin cheese, brown rolls and drinking red wine! Oh lord!

He read Plato to me and poetry. I couldn't tell you whom as I was enraptured by the words, his mouth and his lips! A beautiful memory. That was what poetry meant to me then; beauty, love, lips and mouths. (The precursor to a later fascination with theatre and my creation of The Poet Mouth).

At home, there was little time for poetry, many family arguments over chips, chocolate or tidying up, and very few books. I was an avid reader in my school library, the local lending library, and by nine, was reading books in the adult library adjacent to Queen Mary's College Faculty of Science and Engineering. I wasn't looking for poetry books, but I would stay there for hours.

My 'posh friend' at school Cathy lived in Toynbee Hall, Aldgate East, and there were heaps of books, silence, classical music or Kate Bush on the record player. I spent two years in their lounge near books and music whenever I had the opportunity. We were very close and I was supported by her and her mum tremendously. I remained friends when she moved out of London and began to write my own poetry and they listened to my early poems and encourgaed me.

·· • •• • •• ••·

I'd left school at fifteen after becoming pregnant with simply a boy that I fell for and had no time to write, read or do anything between washing terry towelling nappies, hanging them on the line and cooking dinner. The relationship was not to last. My life was like a re-run of the film Educating Rita, when I attended the local adult education institute to return to learning and by the time my daughter was three, I simply had to leave. My 'posh friend' and her mum helped me with this too.

·· • •• • •• ··

When I was only nineteen, after leaving a friend's house to walk a short distance to my father's, I was attacked in the street by a stranger. My relationship with poetry began properly after this event. My agoraphobia began properly after this event too. Poetry saved me! In the savagery that had occurred, I was able to 'castrate in verse' all that experience. The 'survivor odes' came too, and the healing growth and thriving were soon penned. I was cathartically exorcising every demon and other less troublesome experiences through poetry.

At twenty, I met Tom (God-Love-Him), at my local theatre, The Half Moon in Stepney Green. We fell in love; he wrote poetry about me. I may have written some for him too. He was educated at Radley College Oxford and was dark, like Demetrius, but in 1990 I decided I was *going to be* a lesbian, left Tom (God-Love-Him), whom I loved and wrote about that too. I loved women for fourteen years and was in a women's band, writing song lyrics and gigging across the LGBT scenes. The lyrics for these songs came from my poems. I then decided I wasn't going to be lesbian anymore.

Whilst studying counselling at Uni and exploring themes on sexuality it clicked, years later, that I still loved Tom (God-Love-Him)! I wrote poetry about that, too, went online, nervously set up a dating profile, and began dating men.

·········

I met a well-educated, well-spoken chap living in Oxford, we fell in love, and I soon moved in with him in Oxford in a chocolate box cottage. I wrote no poetry. The relationship turned from love, and after five years, I left to live in a women's refuge. There I wrote songs and was by then a freelance consultant working in an online domestic violence awareness campaign.

I met David, a campaign supporter, who would later be my husband, and we spent ten years in love, performing music and songwriting, and were happily married. We moved from London to Tewkesbury. I thought the house was an idyll for a writer. I sang songs, cooked dinners and was, he said, 'the perfect wife'. I wrote no poetry; I was in love.

··•••••···

I was destroyed after my husband died, and then I wrote poetry.

··•••••···

I began the writing of this book about that grief, set up a poetry page, 'This Shite Grief,' now called 'Tish Ince Poet Writer' on Facebook, joined The Gloucestershire Poetry Society and simply had to perform. It was an urgent emergence!

I've been published internationally and performed poetry at live poetry events before and during Lockdown and globally in Zoom rooms in the UK, United States, Australia, Paris, Japan, Singapore and India.

·········

In Dec 2022, I was nominated for The Pushcart Prize -Best of The Small Presses for my grief poem on the Ukraine War, I Polish Shoes - This is the US's most honoured literary series in America. I am so grateful and honoured to have been nominated.

I'm still isolated, agoraphobic, not driving yet, and a widow. However, I have realised that loss and grief have been my most tearful yet creative times. Poetry and I are emerging, **becoming** much more than I had ever imagined. I am to its feel wings, the span and life, and I'm proud to nurture it. I think my husband would be very proud too.

An early poem after he died, but fitting.

Poetry buds bloom
late in my autumnal
it permeates to fight
finding light, yet my
darkness is a softer
hue of grey
the lips and mouths
words tumble out
in 'will not go'
and 'here to stay'.

Tish Camp - Poet, Writer - 29/01/2020

Chapter Sixteen

Tears – Tech – Teenagers and Trials

Nov 14th 2018

I am crying...I am giving the biggest tears at hubby's picture, rolling on my side, staring at it. I cleaned it earlier today, said good morning, smiled, and set off for my humongous, achievement-laden day. It *will* be an 'achievement day' as I've been setting myself up to be the best of the best at everything; for myself and my kid, grandkids, my friends and my new ventures.

So, at 8.20am, I am ready, having smoked a ciggie, necked a coffee and not one tear in sight. No tears, not today. We are working, and working is a 'hard lady' day. No prisoners, 'get the job done kinda day. My brain is working like it's never worked before. Well, of course, it has, and it did. It had worked very well. But since David died, it went to mush and has not been of much use, too sodden with tears, mouldy old tears that never dry out, that never get that musky smell rid, never get hoovered up with Shake 'N' Vac.

Huge crying befalls me, and I am on a bed with nothing but a picture to hold and my sides in case they spill out. I let the tears fall, rolling off my cheek. I am days away from my widowhood anniversary. I hear a howl emerging from the side that didn't split. The belly houses a wolf with a gargantuan voice. And it whimpers, a growl inside the cavern of me, circling to find the opportunity to out, and I am weak now. I cannot control it.

"GrrrmmmmMMMMHHHHHHHHhhhuuUUUuah-hhhhh"!

He is out, and I am wounded, weak, unable to stop or care to stop his clawing escape from the belly, the cavern of deepest cuts.

········

Tech - 23rd November 2018

Backing up the iPhone is the worst feeling. Again, I need help getting my brain working. Messages are popping up asking me to

"DO something!"

Do something? Do the simple, for others, something that makes me freeze. I hover my hands over a keyboard and am stuck in floods of tears and that expectation that ***I'm going to lose all my history with Dave.***

All my pictures that were 6578 at last count when I, somewhere, had seen a number, but can't recall how I saw that, and why it just doesn't compute that the Cloud is a safe safe, for all my Dave history, pictures and videos. The cloud, where he last looked up, through an ambulance window on our way to the hospice, this time two years ago.

"Or was it one year ago? What year was it?"

That I stood still in this fear. In this unfathomable, fucking fear. The fear of what we'd been told. And how to now live, what little of our lives we had left. Yes, mine too. I was living just prior to his diagnosis, and now I am half lived, half caring, half crying, half hysterical in the life of fear I have now.

Fear of pain and the actual memories I'm now desperate not to lose.

Dave is not talking. I hear hardly anyone talking, just warm words gentle and soothing and reassuring and detailed and able to help brain cells *all cried out*, and that I still needed for me to get this task done. The iPhone 5s, not even sold anymore by iPhone, is holding my life up with fear, In every message of

"Not enough storage."

Or,

"This phone has not been backed up."

In how many months? I have to get another iPhone to begin living my life again. To get used to the technology, I would have breezed through.

"Dave, you're not talking to me,"

I say as I stub out my cigarette into the ashtray. I open the grief book to write. As I do, the iPhone rings, with the name closest to Dave's. Steve, blues buddy, loving friend and caregiver at the very end.

"Steve!

You always do it", I say as he speaks over me.

"I'm sorry, love. I just thought I'd ring you; you've been on my mind."

"Been on your mind? No, you always call *just* when I need it. Dave made you call. I was just in bits then Steve, even saying, Dave, you're not talking to me, then you call. Like Dave saying, 'no babes, ***I'm not talking***, but I'll send Steve."

We talk of a friend that's ill in hospital, Dave's Blues buddy and harmonica player, Bill, and I promise I will visit him before I hang up.

I was pledged to a lift from Gloucester, but that never occurred, and I should have gone somehow earlier, on my own. But I eventually managed to see him; when I heard, he was still in the hospital.

········

I spoke to Dave while walking the twenty-minute walk from home and getting soaked through in flooding rains. I see Bill and bring him the Christmas bag of goodies and visit on my way to get the coach to London on Christmas Eve.

"Babes, I'm on my way to see Bill. Yeah, I got it. You sent Steve a message to call me as you wanted him to be visited and for me to do the Christmas bag. I'm so sorry I didn't get there earlier. I'm just so sorry."

He doesn't answer.

The rain washes away my sins. Of the demanding I should have done or sought help elsewhere, and the strain of knowing I was now making this journey there and onward to London was enough in the guilt I had and the freezing wetness seeping through the puffer jacket into my skin.

I walked the walk of shame with apologies and our tradition of dropping off a Christmas bag to one another homes was still had. I had a bag of bottled beers, Christmas chocolates, biscuits and more. This was his friend, and

"I should have done more. I should have. "

·····•·•••··

Bill was so pleased to see me. I take off the wet coat and hug Bill as he's sat up in bed eating cornflakes at 8.30pm in the evening. We sit and talk, and I'm sorry to see him in such a sad state. We are connected through grief and Dave. This may be the last time I see him as he will be transferred back home, and I may not be able to get to his village as I still don't drive.

Soon I get up and tell him I have to get the coach, and he looks so pleased that I have come, and I leave and walk to the coach stop.

"I saw him, Dave. I saw him. He looked so pleased about the bag and said he was bringing one for us when he gets out."

I wanted him to say,

"Well done."

He was at least quiet. But I knew the visit wasn't about me and my guilt. It was about *him* and *his* friendship and wanting his friend to know **he was there** too.

As I stood in the rain, I began to understand this silence. He was with me on the coach as soon as we pulled out of Tewkesbury, and I looked out of the window and held his hand, none of us speaking.

·········

Baby Pneumonia

My grandchildren were always, and are, my world. Our marriage featured them regularly during the summer, Easter and Christmas holidays and many visits to our home for these breaks and babysitting in London.

The youngest was born after David died, and I missed him, but at a freezing cold weekend, he was ill, and a series of doctors and hospital visits proved the cold he'd had a week earlier was much more than that. The Calpol and Ibuprofen suggested without antibiotics created hard pockets of mucus in one of his lungs, and he was finally, and at much insistence on my and his mother's part, diagnosed at the hospital with this and pneumonia.

It was nine days, two hospital transfers for specialist support, and the longest wait before the fever broke, and he was declared over the worst but would remain with weakened lungs. We prayed to Dave and all spiritual support constantly. Facebook friends also prayed, and the Cheltenham Reiki group helped with distant Reiki for the baby. The fever broke just after this, and I was delighted to share his return to health pics soon after .. Bless everyone for this fantastic effort.

....

Teenagers

My older teenage grandson, during this period, came to stay at my home in the countryside after having problems in London. He was a comfort and was admittedly a struggle, but both of us were at least together. I would be now, clearly **cooking again!**

I made up house, school and street rules that he tried his hardest to meet, sent him to school each day, and banged on bathroom doors to get him out of the shower into school and finally into his first job!

It was a joy to buy a high-vis jacket, safety helmet, and safety shorts for the landscaping work he'd found.

The delivery of new safety boots was going to be a few days late, so there was a rush to find some quickly. I had sent David's clothes, shoes and work gear all by now to the local hospice charity shop and didn't expect to see any boots anywhere. But in the top cupboard where the heavy tools and circular saw were kept, was a pair of Dave's steel-toe capped boots I'd missed, that were precisely his size! Almost as if they were meant for him, for this moment.

Dave was *telling me* and the boy that he was around, with the very thing he would have been looking for to save some money and the **grandparent manly thing** he would have done.

The last time they were together, Dave taught him how to chop logs in the wooded area out the back. I stood proudly watching this transition into young manhood, this glorious man-to-boy moment with my semi-faux

"Oooh, be careful"

and lovingly,

"Wow, look at you!"

as the boy swung the splitter firmly like Dave had taught him.

That was three days before Dave was diagnosed with the brain tumour, **before all our lives were forever changed**, and for me, a clear timeline to the beginnings of this boy's own grief and his own unspoken pains and walk into **'the without fields.'**

The boots symbolised another transition that Dave was indeed present for and another gift and *life after affirmation* he left.

"Grandpa Dave would be so proud of you. If he could see you now?"

I said to him. My grandson just looked so proud of himself and the boots. I looked at Dave's picture on the top of the piano.

"Hey, Dave! Look at this boy. Looking good, huh?"

I wanted him to be proud of him and me, and he most definitely was. My smiling grandson looked so proud, too, and I felt his self-esteem shoot through the ceiling, along with my love for him and Dave.

············

He was with me for over two years, and eventually, he returned to his mother's in London. He is happy to be back home with his family, baby brother and the annoying little sister he loves and looks out for. And my grandson is proud of me too.

Chapter Seventeen

Widow Dating – and Patio Doors

Widow Dating – 2020

So, I think I may be ready to do this widow dating thing as a new thing I can do. Having heard my dead husband say he was leaving me (for fucks sake) again and that it was time to move on. And having had an eighteen-month hiatus with the man that ended the way it did, I decided I would try to spend time with other widowers or men who were understanding about widowhood and maybe just wanted coffee.

Yes, you read that right, men that just want coffee? How naïve does one need to be to think that men just want to have coffee? There is a time when every woman wonders,

"Are we just friends?' Should we stay just friends,"

or

"Will we get this shit together and hit the hay?"

If she does not ask these questions, she definitely considers something or someone else altogether. I embarked on a tirade of events and happenings that had me reeling into the dark and murky world of widow dating. And whom this world benefits, the liars, the cheats and the downright bed hoppers that want to ensure you are readily available or the

"Might just jolly well start crying"

which will cue his sharp exit, that he probably wanted all along.

"Phew. close call."

No, this is a world of feigned empathy, black bra and knickers, tissues in dressing gown pockets, vulnerability, guilt, pictures of dead husband on bedside cabinets, or turned over, or taken from the bedroom and put on coffee tables.

Or, reimagined in your head, hearing noises in rooms or by the front door, and getting out of bed to go see, when you just want to not be in bed, feeling different skin, different bones, different smells and different faces. Even if you close your eyes, the reimagined face is now looking at you projected onto the bedroom door, ceiling curtains or any flippin where you look. Then next to the reimagined face of your dead husband, you're angry at the intrusion from both.

Guilty about the 'affair', it feels like you're having, amongst the imploding, exploding unresolved grief orgasm that is nearly always just out of reach.

I lost the sexuality I had when he died, and now widow dating has its rules that I do not yet, understand. What I do understand is the excruciating conflict we widows are in with these issues to contend with. And the still, absolute and authentic expression of declaring a physical need for human touch, companionship and fighting our no-strings-fun personas that we are seemingly thrown into in the bull pit, pissy, shitty world that it can be.

What widows find is that they can cry a lot before, sometimes during and often after such interactions, even online with men. Lying men that are trying very hard to be *genuine* on *their* widow profiles for a sympathy fuck or *are* real but are equally just as broken as you are and still want and need to meet someone for the said contact and companionship.

·····•·•••··

I joined a widow dating website and filled out a profile with the hopes that I could simply meet someone for a coffee and make new friends to be in the presence of other men. Besides the company of my dead husband that, as I said, I carried about in the rucksack or had in tow. My conversations with him over this were always one-sided.

Just a little before this, I'd met **The Cool Crowd** in Town at a music event that was altogether zany as fuck, and I really liked them. Another choirmaster/hippie chick, a couple of musicians, and some happy women danced and danced and welcomed me to join in too.

"So, erm, I'm going out, Dave," I told him. "There's a group I've made friends with, and they're really kinda cool, and this guy offered me a coffee if ever I was in town, so, erm...."

Dave didn't reply, just watched me, sometimes standing by the chest of drawers at others, pretending to look interested in the squeaky hinge on the wardrobe door or the broken handle on the pine dressing table. Like he was thinking about doing D.I.Y. I'd repeat again till I knew I'd gotten his attention.

I knew this was me checking out if I really did **have his blessing** and bless him, he tried so hard to give it, but his eyes were always wide, deferred to some piece of wood and trying to look non-plussed, under the hurt.

I was really still very hurt by him. So, we play the game, not showing each other that we're pissed at the other and that we're all OK with shit.

Dave would watch me getting dressed, showering (yes, I was at least getting clean by then), and blow-drying my hair, and I tried my hardest to be gentle and careful about his feelings. Putting make-up on and fixing to spray perfume.

"But I always wore perfume daily, so he shouldn't worry about me trying to impress anyone."

But there was a part of me that was very much,

"Look, you said you wanted me to move on, so I'm sorry if this is painful (no, I wasn't), but I have to look OK now going out to an actual real live place. A coffee shop or a bar, and yeah, if someone finds me attractive, so be it. After all, this is what *you said* **you wanted?**"

This whole conversation was in my own head, but I knew if he could walk through walls, turn up whenever, and be inside me or in a rucksack of grief, then he'd also be able to be inside my head and hear my thoughts and probably answer me right in there too.

·· • • • • • • ··

In the 'room inside my head', there is a duplicate dressing table, and we *are* actually talking. However he's now like an ex-partner but still, very close friend that cares about me and must have split up with me but would still worry about the next dude that comes along and if I'm going to be OK.

In this room, he lives in my house, we're like flatmates, and he gets daily updates and is a free spirit. Ha, yes, a free spirit, just as am I. We can do what we want in our own rooms and lives, but we split the bills, eat couscous together, and read The Guardian on Sundays.

In this flat share, he doesn't bring anyone home with him. He has no girlfriend after me and is ever watchful or pissed that he dumped me, knowing full well I won't take him back, that I'm ever pissed at him and that *I* will jolly well keep on doing what he *told me to do*, in a self-sabotage kind of way.

"No, I'm not rubbing it in."

Oh gosh, every time I say those words or write those words, I remember the suntan oil and the Greek holiday love-ins and yes,

"Where was I?"

See how these triggers come? I digress,

"Yes, rubbing it in. No, I'm not doing that. But I'm clearly playing some still-pissed-at-you game."

In this increasingly student flatshare, not professionals flatshare (that will come later). No, this student flatshare, I am wearing the clothes I want to wear, leaving coffee cups on the coffee table without a coaster, losing the remote frequently and eating and running to

"The life he wanted me to have, for fucks sake."

A little life, a hopeful but still **very little life.** I'm still pissed at him, and he

"Won't get to hug me in *my bed* because I will likely have another man in it, so fucking there, Dave! And you'll be where? I don't know, but I'll probably **meet you in the hall with an oversized tee shirt, no knickers, and a cigarette in my mouth.**"

These are the back-at-you games I play out, act out, in my head with him, that I so dearly want him to see, and

"Yes, I *am* fucking rubbing it in. You left me, fucker."

So, I'm back, out of the *room in my head,* into the actual bedroom. He's looking for an imaginary screwdriver to feign busyness.

"So, erm, yes, I'll be back later, and I'm really looking forward to going for a coffee in town, and hey, I'm riding the bike again!"

I try to look flighty. But damn, this man knows me, I'm hurt, but he just can't speak and wants me to *be* with him. Maybe for *me* to ask for *him* back, to make *him* feel wanted again

"I do fucking want you." (quiet thought)

to soothe *his* jealousy, his 'not-allowed-spirit-got-the green-eye-on-me', he really can't. And it's like, I know the rules too, and I'm holding him in this purgatorial power tripping, hurt bitch, rerun, no one being authentic with each other shit.

He can't speak.

and he is not allowed to go back on his declaration. We are kind of divorced. Divorced flatmates. And my lipstick on is the last straw.

··········

Costa Coffee Date

So, off I go, wheeling my way into town and coffee-ing myself into Costa, cappuccino, big cupping my way into the same seat I sat in opposite my alive then, husband and the anxiousness begins.

I am trying very hard to sit through it and play with brown sugar crystals spilt onto the tabletop, elbows in, Catholic flagellation homily, and feeling like each crystal is a nail from the crucifixion, heavy wooden arms I carry around with me.

Change space now....change space now! Get up, woman and change the space you're in right the hell now.

I do, and I just manage to get outside before the big tears beneath my sunglasses fill up in the bucket of tiny shoal tears that are about to be sploshed down my cheeks.

Damn it, darn and blast these tears. They are just as heavy as my arms. I breathe it out and light a cigarette and sit outside at a table.

I can people-watch, but not people-speak, fully. I need to be more able and ready to meet people. The coffee people. The young office workers, the elderly couples or the disabled electric mobility scooter people, but given a shot, they are the safest bet.

"It's warm today, huh?"

Forced out in twelve-year-old choir boy unmodulated pitch that drops viciously quickly into a male tenor teen in a bedroom, caught looking at porn

"Get out my room mum" tones.

They have their own sugar crystal arms and lives, stay silent, and I leave them be. I am still very full of the hopes of connection that are so much like a flashing beacon down the road of fuck-it-up highway, and I berate myself and assess myself all at once.

I play with my phone and hold onto the bike, needing to adjust pannier straps for absolutely no clear-to-onlookers reason. I feel the anxiety kick in again and play with my cigarette lighter. In these situations, people generally call a friend, look at Facebook, or text someone.

It's lunchtime still, and sunshine and a woman walking towards me smiling. I am frightened but smile back, and they approach, walk past me and sit with their friend who looks like she hasn't had anyone die on her yet and has clean hair that flows nicely in the wind.

I am crushed at my attempt, the foolishness that a stranger smiling and walking towards me was offering free smiles and a V.I.P. ticket to her life. Which I would have gladly taken just to observe and learn from.

I sit for some time, shy and anxious, and red in my ears.

"Someone's talking about me!"

Yep, that's right, Miss V.I.P Table, and the smiled at, stirred coffee, as I glanced like a stupid crazy woman that just smiled back for

"No fucking reason, no fucking fuck's sake reason? Yes, that's what you just did, you stupid, shit-faced, Billy-No-Mates, fuck."

I am stopped by the continued negative self-talk by music just blasting out through a sound system from the busker with an electric organ and his setting up. I stroke my bike's leather handlebars again

"For no apparent fucking reason"

and

"All of this is and looks stupid."

But my distraction has a life of its own. One more cigarette, and I am up and watching this man play all sorts, and now Miss V.I.P. table guests are smiling and saying

"Aww,"

at the songs, and now they're nodding towards me and

"Smiling at me. At me! At me!! With me!!!"

We are throwing smiles around, and I get over-excited and have to reign it in and look away. The human connection is so close I can hear its heartbeat. He plays a song that I know, and I just do the craziest thing and start singing along with his music. I sing for myself and my dead husband and for all widows everywhere.

And the fuck-sake dressing gowns and tissues worldwide, all the knickers not worn or left in the laundry, leggings that don't fit and empty packets of noodles I feel all at once, across the globe. I am singing defiantly to God and flipping him the finger.

I am alive, and I survived and am surviving even this, and this song is my grief overcome in my fight back and into the street. On this high street I live and the people that like it for two minutes and the keyboard busker that nods along with my beat, my broken heartbeat, and soul-shattered crescendos. I say to the man,

"Thank you"

and feel like I have orgasmed or something.

··········

I wheel my bike up the road and leave for the walk back home with Dave, and me sobbing on the bike path and stepping on a snail.

"Are you O..?"

"No, I'm NOT, Dave. I'm not! See? I told you! I knew it was all too much trying to get out like this, it's all because you told me to, and if I was back at home with you, I wouldn't have to deal with this or be like this and what the fuck am I doing in this town? Where the fuck is my life going? I told you, I told you, I fucking told you…huu..hu..huu."

He's almost wheeling the bike with me and trying to steady it while I'm in a rage, wanting to throw

"That fucking bike."

in the bushes or over a railway bridge, something dramatic and painful. The bike – the happy blue vintage bike he bought me, the happy bike, the happy, happy, happier than me bike. The joyful floral panniers, the wicker basket, the bell, the country rides, the memories, the smell of summer, and the wind in my clean hair. The grass and the apples, the grandkids on bikes with us, the car-boot sales and dirt-cheap bikes for a tenner, the hot dogs, the mustard, scorching hot tea, bags of hot mini doughnuts just cooked. The laughing. The laughing, the music on the radio, the singing in the car with him, with them, unloading the bikes and watching these not-here kids ride them around the grounds. The bumble bee summers and lemonade and lavender days. These memories stab so cleverly at my heart.

· · · • · • · · ·

I am home. He is behind me, almost taking my bag from me, quiet and following a few steps behind in case I throw something at one of the walls and watches me throw my fat angry arse into my end of the sofa. Still in my 'going out made an effort' clothes, summertime scarf and warm fleecy grey jacket.

I put my arms around myself, a hand on my stomach, and one wrapped over my boob and into my armpit. I lay with tissues grabbed from these pockets, pick up the black mascara off hot cheeks and down to my nose, and blow. He's trying to offer the remote. I pick it up with one foot from his end of the sofa, flick it up towards my thigh, bring my knees up and stay there, eyes only up to select something. Anything to stop these head-splitting sofa sessions. A movie to fall asleep to at four in the afternoon. A death, widow film. Something gentle, where she walks off or drives off into a sunset, knowing she's going to be OK. I drift into sleep at my foetal end, and he lifts my feet at his and gently sits down, holding them in his hands.

"Are we ever going to talk about him coming back home and staying?"

I ask myself into the sleep of sleeps. The sleep that will bring carpets of forget-me-nots and cartoon Disney worlds of pinks and yellows. Auburn-haired girls that slay dragons with arrows and wicked stepmothers that are just too wicked, too akin to sister grief to watch. I sleep into these dreams, and he joins me. I am a smiling woman. In this animated bubble gum and strawberry sundae cups, of nothing hurts you here, fun.

He dances with me, like Beauty and the Beast or Cinderella at the ball. He sweeps me off my feet into a candy-floss sky, and we ride marshmallow roller coasters into his nirvana. I am gentle, and he is holding my hand. We laugh, and all feels as it should in the world. In this world where I so want to stay. Where there are no wet days, no wet cheeks, no pallets of grey, and all is pastel balloons and cream and raspberry trifle.

·······•·•·······

I wake up cold and have just begun to realise that I will wet myself If I don't jump up now and head for the loo. These traumatic days bring a return to remembered traumas all their own, and a switch is tripped that says you are not safe. It is dark in the house, save the light in the kitchen and bathroom. I am hungry and look at my phone while I'm on the toilet. Three text messages.

"I tried to call."

"What happened?"

"Are you OK?"

The new friend, a coffee date that didn't happen. A bad signal and a crazy woman returns home. I don't answer. I watch the T.V. in my bedroom, get into bed with all my made-an-effort clothes on and sleep till morning. I woke up the next morning, and I was better. The social anxiety that keeps me home now, along with the widow coffee date gone wrong, generic agoraphobia, and

"Got to make an effort"

clothes, is enough to put a dressing gown back on and stay on. I am gentle with myself, coaxing positive self-talk reruns of the smiling V.I.P. girl, and

"The whole world doesn't know what's happened to me? The smiled-at-other may have possibly had someone die on her"

and all that seems much more balanced and actually more believable and forgiving of me.

"Forgiving. Forgiving. Hmmm. This is my day to forgive the world."

Forgive the world for its carry-on-living, for smiling or listening to the radio. Or laughing along with their T.V. For going shopping, eating ice cream in the sun. For picnics, for having husbands alive, for catching Frisbees, for riding bikes with families, for answering calls with smiles on faces, for going out to discos, managing to be at work, for being able to eat full meals, for buying salads when they don't have dead husbands. For coffees in car parks, watching through windscreens on promenades in Cornwall, for dressing up in glitter or down in leggings that fit for D.I.Y. or housework. For cleaning when no one is visiting. For making cupcakes, buying shampoo, using shampoo, cleaning their shoes, and buying ridiculous high-priced items of no significant or life-affirming value at Amazon.

For

"Not needing others, not needing others, for not needing anything."

And finally,

"For being jolly well grown up about this death thing."

·· · • • • • • • • ··

I put the P.A. on, a karaoke machine he bought me for my 50th Birthday, and crank it up loud. Ten minutes of the Lightness of Being Green Tara, mantra healing music on YouTube, comes blasting through the house. It's an energy all its own and feels like a huge bucket of light being sloshed into all corners with a fabulous mop of chakra colours, slopping around the nooks and crannies with hot, positively charged love-bubbles water. Now, I am in my Disney clean-up film, Snow White style. A physical clean-up and I'm alone and have no need for the birds, or bunny rabbits helping, the dwarfs or anyone to rescue me from the Grief Witch, that came to choke me on her 'apple of alone.' I am sloshing and cleaning the nooks and crannies of me psychically too. To remove all negative energy and thoughts. Soul spiked with too many purple heart emojis right into the core of The Black Widow,

The Abyss of Still and the tumultuous Rapids of Without White Water Canyon, set to either drown me quickly or slowly. I prefer slow. I digress, but I noted the

"Just popped by"

Sally Suicide that just came calling.

"Yes, yes, OK! For fuck's sake, now I have a friend?"

The door slams and she looks hurt. She brought a bottle of some cheap booze too.

"Oh, fuck off, Sally. Now, now. I'm supposed to be positive. I'll call her later and apologise, maybe text, as I don't want to give the wrong impression. Fuck this empathic. Just tell her to, argh! Back to positive, girl!! Yes, yes, The psychic cleaning."

Away from all that dark and dirty, dank and smelly, and downright deliberation in depression.

"I am cleaning myself up! So, let's start with some inside work!!! "

The music lifts every slice of festering, mouldy bread in the bottom of my *insides fridge*. From me and away from me. I throw away the bacteria sponge infecting the kitchen top surface and sing along. It's even better when you do!

'Ek Ong Kar

Sat Gur Prasad

Sat Gur Prasad

Ek Ong Kar'

Over and over again until the cleaning and the psychic mop and bucket are placed on the side. And I'm grabbing my first self-care cappuccino with chocolate on top for a ciggie outside. The real life, birds and the bees and the odd butterfly come look at

"What's going on?"

passing through open patio doors, and I let them. A few passing neighbours walking their dogs or reading outside also note

"What's happening?"

and give me a nod, or if their widowed, ask,

"Is it a good day?"

and I say,

"Good MORNING!"

like a well-paid singing postman, proudly adjust my dressing gown cord and say

"YES!'

Now I'm ready to get showered and plan actual clothes to wear.

"Yep, real clothes. It's gonna be a good day."

I start to sing in the shower songs of my youth and wash that hair until my plus size Loreal audition, *because I'm worth it*, wins me the role in the parody remake of South Pacific'

"Gonna wash that grief right outa my hair"

and I'm whisked off to make-up for day one shooting! I sit at the dressing table, put make-up on, blow dry my hair again, light lipstick, spray my perfume on, and then, then...yes...then!

"Then, then..then.."

Lower and lower tones. The bass of me. The slow drum begins. Remembering

"I'm getting ready to go out with him."

The tears fall, and I'm black mascara face and back on the bed looking at his picture, numb or crying or both, in turns, until I fall asleep again. It's probably six hours or so before I wake up again. These catch-ups. Sleeps that my body just throws me into because of not sleeping the night, and nights and ongoing nights, before.

···•••••···

Patio Doors

The cool afternoon air curls into the bedroom's open door like a gnarly finger of smoke, beckoning me to sit with him in the front room. He enters through patio doors that look scared at this intruder and give me a look that said,

"We tried to wake you,"

I'm annoyed at the doors but still say,

"It wasn't your fault. It's alright, I got this."

The Patio Doors are like twelve-year-old twins, caring for me, taking responsibility for me because that's what I asked for. That's what I demanded, and they complied. They

"Weren't equipped to take this on."

This return to me and my childhood. Caring for my mum in her grief,

"I wasn't equipped to take that on."

I resist the Gnarly Finger Smoke, and he is Will of the Whisp, gone. **This house.** That is really me. **The rooms of me.** My psyche, my edge of awareness, or becoming aware. My awareness in and of each. And my consciousness reached or noted. My

"Becoming clear."

My reflections of who I am now, then, and will be, hoped for in the Looking Glass. The childhood

"Alice Band I loved about my head, my long hair, and my little fringe when mum took care of me before she left."

I think about a child of similar age, my granddaughter and make a much-needed phone call.

Chapter Eighteen

Co-Dependency – Family Grief and Days of the Dead

4th November 2022

It's my granddaughter's birthday. I rang her this morning to say happy birthday; she was already a teenager. I look back at my youth and what I was like as a teenager, and this afternoon I've been thinking about that more.

I was posting my new website link, and a poet mentioned it was a really good site and said it's amazing how much I've endured and how I've come back from that. I got quite tearful this afternoon, processing what that meant for me.

I leant over and thanked my husband just for loving me, and I felt very poignant about my youth and some of the losses there. And he encouraged me and reassured me that now was the right time. I wouldn't have been able to have written all that I had if I hadn't experienced all that I had, and I'm grateful for that worldly advice.

However, I think about the things that I still need to resolve. I think about my upset at my first husband's death, my annoyance about the plans I had for my life and how they were almost thrown into the coffin with him. I was so angry with him. I was so upset because the rest of my life with him and what I had hoped for my life, I believed, would never be realized now that he'd died. And there was a point where I'd said.

"Don't worry, I'll be able to grieve. I won't be like a child grieving, like feeling abandoned"

But indeed, I have been, and I always have been. From the original abandonment, from when my mother left when I was six years of age, and I don't think I've quite gotten over that. So, of course. I'll process the loss of my late husband in those terms too. I look at the vulnerability that I've had and what that's always meant for me.

During the five-year part-time person-centred counselling course, we would have had to have counselling with co-students and tutors before we went out as student counsellors. After many hours of counselling, I believed that I had dealt with those abandonment issues, but quite frankly, I don't think I have, and that's why his death felt like a complete 'leaving me.' So, I looked at all of this as a counsellor and processed my progress in grief.

··•••••••··

Co-Dependency

I can see I've become co-dependent on my dead husband, not letting him go, with my internal screaming and my insistence with him whenever he's ever spoken to me, telling me he has to go. And anger at the loss, which I've always known inside, felt like my child, *The Child* in me. And that goes to the original source, which is my mother leaving me.

"So yeah! Co-dependent on a dead husband."

There's a lot of work to be done, and the clarity I'm having now around this makes me feel stronger, older and wiser. Makes me feel nervous about letting go. I know for healthy grieving; I know I must. So, I'm angry all over again that there's another learning curve that I have to go through.

This is just the first layer. There'll be many more tears for that original loss, which I can deal with.

··•••••••··

Family Grief

We are told that it is healthy to grieve together as a family, but what of separated families? What of the ability to sit or cry together in a divorced household? A Mum's or Dad's house, filled with grief but parked between two visits and an array of dynamics of siblings that may be caught up in favouring one parent over another. Or adult children that are too busy to sit with elderly parents. Families that are not together in different countries and time zones.

I was eleven when my sister Helen died. She was seventeen. We were thrown into grief and shock, and trauma. A tragedy that split my father's heart with an axe. I was shocked to see his shoulders drop and form a space so hollow I didn't believe a body could turn so slowly and undeniably concave and still hold space for his organs.

I saw this metamorphosis and understood grief was *inside*, captured forever and would be the sad prisoner he did not want. There would be no bars, no fight for freedom, no roof riots, no smashing up cells, smearing of shit on any walls, no upturned mattresses, and no fighting with other inmates. Just sad, cornered grief, on the floor unfed, tired, hopeless and waiting to die.

My mother was to be told on a telephone call, and I recall the Irish tale of the Banshee coming to warn of death. I remember the story of the Banshee's sound and heard grief like this in my mam. I watched her grief as if a raging wolf, with a leg bloodied and dragging a rusted trap along the ground forever. Whimpering into the snow and the ever-after. The body turned even more inward than my fathers' as grief grew in age with her, and her head stooped more readily into both alcohol and then, later, a bible.

After Jean, our next sister's death in 1986, and later in 1994 when Christine, our eldest sister, died, we were lost once more in our hardened and able approach to funeral parlour payments. We adult children had learned and grown enough to now take over the preparations for funerals and payments and orders of service with and for a mum and dad, two separated and joined forever in this unholy return to loss of child, grief.

I grew less. Less in my uttered wants and needs, the asking for and of each parent, and learned how to grow in an untended grief garden. Weeds would form around me, and it was hard to flourish like that. My grief would be on the back-burner until mum and dads' were tended to in separate ways. I would reverse roles and parent them as needed, as grief was experienced in their own unique ways.

·····•·••··

When grief straightens up a body again against all odds, implores its goaler-come-prisoner a leave to remain, and pardons us for a while, only a while, to get jobs done, kids to school, work to continue, we are grateful. These are the days of achieving, overcoming, and escaping grief's power over us. We are both nervous and able to walk from the cells of our crouched and bent positions. Our bare feet tread across terrains that would cut, make bleed and turn anyone back to seated to inspect. But there is a pain far more searing inside our becoming, the willing of our core strengthened chests, that **the path is bearable.** The blood is colour; for our grey, the wounds are undoubtedly less.

·····•·••··

During the hiatus between deaths, lighting candles, and praying, I maybe attended spiritualist churches occasionally with siblings or with mum, seeking that Netherworld contact. I would initially deny these moments of spiritual connection and, as the years went by and I accepted them, would be entirely grateful for them. Some are as funny as fuck, and one that I will tell here is about my mum and my late husband, most contact coming through with him and her after he died.

So, when mam died, and David was sick, I was already open to hearing from her. In fact, using an Irish accent was a valuable way to help him talk.

"Ah, David, as me mudder would say, would ya like a bowl of porridge and are you wanting a coppa tea?"

Usually had him laughing at the breakfast table when I was after him hurrying before a chemo visit. He liked the musicality of the accent, and he spoke more when I was like this. Trying to get him safely from the shower one day, I knocked on the bathroom door as we were travelling soon in the hospital transport, and we'd have to be ready for the pick-up time. As I knocked louder still, I said,

"Please, David, we need to get a move on."

He replied something along the lines of

"Yes when I'm ready!"

At this point, I heard my mother's voice say,

"Ah, leave the man alone!"

I was shocked but went with it.

"Ah, see now David? I just heard my mam say "Ah, leave the man alone!" She was always on your side when she was alive, and now look, still on your side!"

He laughed out loud and then came out.

·····•·····

Days of The Dead - Dead Party

(Scene – empty from room - my birthday - June 2021)

Me: "I'm calling for this little get-together as Day of the Dead is coming up, and I'm supposed to be sharing something of my experiences with the dead in my life. So, if you would be so kind as to answer this spiritual invitation? Mum? .... David? .....(that's my husband) Dad?" (first-time attendee)

(to camera) It's like I'm anxious about the turnout. No need to worry about sausage rolls in the oven or having enough seats; they all seem to stand in the main.

Me: "Mam?

Mam: "What?" *(she's pissed at being dragged from the repeats on her 24/7 Jerry Springer cloud)*

Me: "Oh...er, good you're here."

Mam: "Yes"

Me: "Where's David?

Mam: "How should I know?"

Me: "Ok, cos lately he's been with you?"

Mam: "Yes, that's because he can't tell you anything without me. I see you're still smoking?"

Me: "Yes, er, yes, I am, *(said more boldly than I'd hoped)* - Er, Mam, I asked Dad to come."

Mam: What's that? What?" *(she softens some and checks her outfit).*

Director note: (*She's always had eyes for him, after all these divorced years and even now, in death. We get interrupted by the phone – A WhatsApp message*)

Daughter: "The kids haven't eaten. Have you got anything? Be there in 20mins x."

(*My daughter is driving up the motorway with two grand-kids, 11 and almost 3 years old, the other 16, living with me*)

Me: "Yes, I'll put hotdogs on x."

(*I watch mum roll her eyes at my choice of food, as I know she thinks "Dat boy could do wid a real meal."*)

Me: "We're going out for my birthday.. table has been booked for 3pm."

(*I say directly to her. I'm getting busy. Butterflies inside my tummy are anxious, but I know my legs are heading towards the kitchen. I want her to follow.*)

Me: "Is David here yet?" (*I know he isn't, but I'm stalling for time*)

Mam: "No, but where's your father?"

(*Dad appears as I'm ripping open finger rolls and getting hotdogs into the frying pan. I get awkward and nod bleakly at him, and feel the rudest of hosts, a red flush rising in my cheeks. He is dead: guest of honour, but these hungry kids and the daughters' tongue. So, I fix up, turn, and greet him appro-priately. He's already seen mum and has a scowl on his face.*)

Me: "Dad, you're here! I'm so glad you could come. I'm sorry, Michelle and the kids are almost here too, and the kids need hotdogs. Dad, I invited mum.?"

Dad: "Yes, I'm here." (*I stand still. Hot dogs sizzle to a slow stop. I've turned the gas off.)*

Dad: "Where's David, Trisha?"

(I bite my annoyed tongue, knowing full well dead or alive, he needs another man to talk to and answer him respectfully)

Me: "Dad, I don't know yet. I'll call him again."

(Mum is watching me. I can't do it properly while people are watching and judging. This is one thing she can't complain about me doing wrong, maybe a bit slow, but the getting busy feelings, dead family dynamic and missing husband situation don't help.)

Me: "David, where are you, babes?"

(I try to hide my annoyance at him not being here on time and secretly tell him that mum and dad are here already! I'm about to ask him to 'pick up juice at the garage for the kids and maybe some ....?' but for the life of me, I don't know what dead people drink now.)

(I'm getting stressed. Mum is looking at family pictures on the piano. Dad is standing like Prince Charles in the kitchen, equally in judgement at the hotdogs, and David finally arrives.)

Me: "David! Oh, for fucks sake." (*I tell him, rolling my eyes back at the parents behind me. He understands.*)

Me: "I don't know where Ellis is, and Michelle is about 3 mins away."

(*He rescues me and takes over the hosting.*)

David: "Helloo," (*he says to both and smiles*)

Dad: "Hello, my friend," dad says to him,

Mam: "Ah, David. Ah, now!"

(*David smiles at mam, too and leads them into the hallway. They are all scootching up by the piano, and I'm back to whacking out hotdogs in finger rolls with tomato sauce. I plate up on a big silver tray and walk through all of them to the front room. I always feel guilty if I've got to dash around the house as these spirits are slow at walking.*)

(*I'm sweating a little but want to take the one minute I have left with them before the doorbell rings, to just be their daughter and his wife. Have them say well done, and don't worry, it's all gonna be fine, and thank **them** for coming. They are still.... I am still. I want to be with them and ask them lots and lots of questions, but I fear this moment will be gone, and the party will have begun.*)

(*Dad nods first; this is enough. David smiles gently and winks his 'you-got-this, wink at me.*)

Director Notes: (*Scene – Laptop - Tish Camp in half lighting from a lamp on a white desk writing time on a laptop is*

22.03pm date 12th October 2021. Typing the Day of The Dead scene. I have an acknowledgement from David. As she writes this, she hears a loud, piercing whistle in her right ear. "Yes, I got this!" she replies.

(back to the front room - The doorbell rings. Mum looks at me and takes a seat on the arm of the big chair. She is soft and encouraging.)

Mam: "Go on now.... we'll see you in a minute."

Chapter Nineteen

Morrisons - Early Grief - Images of my Death - Painting with Bob Ross

I am now more determined than ever to get out of the house and buy food. Not just a slow walk with him beside me to the garage, dragging my old widow shopping trolley behind me and filling it with eggs, bread, milk, Jack Daniels, and coke at the petrol station. I mean real food.

By this, I mean something more than the weightless 29p noodles or sweet and sour chicken microwave meals with four pieces of chicken for £1.00. These pieces of chicken are small as fuck, but I still managed to choke on each piece as I slowly chewed.

Food was the biggest trigger for me. Eating is crucial in a widow's journey. Healthy food, any food, but definitely calories.

I took photographs of this, the trolley, the bus stop in the rain, the heaviness of grief, the awkwardness, the scrawled finger drawing 'bus stop shopping done'.

I took numerous photos to catalogue this grief on the packets of noodles, the ready meals, the Jack Daniels, chocolate and every other numbing thing I could push grief further down my choked-up throat with.

I took photos of the sammiches I'd made, the peanut butter, then slowly cooked meals, two in a week! I progressed to noodles with vegetables and weightless prawns in the early days.

The widows' group online watch me in the photos I'm sharing as I cook at twelve midnight. I plan and cook a grief protein cake. Haha! – coconut flour, chocolate, cocoa powder, walnuts, almonds, anything nutty I could grind down, oil, sugar and need. I waited for it and produced this huge brown heavy protein slab of energy. The energy I needed.

I placed it in the empty fridge and took a photo of that. This would be my salvation. I took a slice and cleaned the house on that cake for a whole week! Then it was gone.

·· • • • • • • ··

I could manage Grief Cake as it had no airs or illusions of family slices and was a product of necessity. I moved my legs quicker and cleaned a bit. Edges of tables, the minimal washing up, threw tissues away, emptied out every fuck-sake dressing gown pocket stuffed with tissues, sofas and tissues, bed strewn with tissues, washed clothes that I hadn't worn or knickers that I had and I believe, hoovered once!

I'd spent thirteen months arranging diets that would be amazing for a health freak but couldn't touch them after he died. There would have been shit loads of antioxidants, blueberries, black kale, dark green, dark or purple vegetables, salads, fish, chicken, lentils, no sugar, and almost all organic.

The meals were six a day. Yes, you read that right, six! Breakfast, mid-morning snack, lunch, afternoon snack, dinner and some kind of supper if he needed it, and boy, did he? The steroids make you hungry as hell.

I cooked, prepared and ate everything with him. These were what made his blood works come back as 'good' and would fortify him and allow him, with such good results, to be strong enough to deal with the next round of chemo.

Yes, six months of chemo and radiation therapy, all for a *maintenance dose,* meaning it was not a cancer-curing treatment; it was already made clear to us there was no curing this. No, this would be to ensure longevity. The prognosis for Glioblastoma is anything from 4 – 14 months, and I was fucked if he was going to die early on me.

I was on a walking stick then after a bad knee injury ten years earlier, and this near killed me. The cooking, preparing and 24-hour supervision of my husband with cognitive impairment was the most stressful experience ever.

So, when I *got* to sit down to eat with him, I damn near choked on every mouthful.

·········

Pre-emptive grief

Pre-emptive grief is a state of, simply put, grieving early. You know he will die, and you are caught up in thoughts of life without him. This is why mindfulness is so important: staying in the moment and just being with the person remaining present.

I was sitting and eating with him or listening to him play his blues guitars, knowing that meant he wasn't wandering off. I choked back tears and food. This was the beginning of a gag reflex that remained for years after, returning whenever I was upset. It didn't feature if I ate cake, however, Lol.

·········

Morrisons continued...

So, I'm venturing out to Morrisons supermarket, and the walk is slow and deliberate. He is beside me, not saying anything, but I'm giving him updates:

"So, I'll get some spinach and eggs and um, milk. Maybe some chicken or something?"

I lied. I also didn't mention the alcohol I wanted. It's like, I know he can probably see everything at any time, but I still feel like I don't want any for-fuck-sake judgements. The store is ominous as I approach. I see fast cars pulling in and pulling out, people walking quickly and then the clear slow stroll of husbands and wives holding hands, getting baskets or pushing trolleys together. That is the hardest. Big boxes of Daz and Persil washing powder greet me like a stained-glass church aisle beckoning me into the cleanliness that I am so far away from with the security guard, a God-like laundromat attendant, jingling change.

He watches me a little, and I feel the stain of my widowhood become grief blood, viewable even through my black leggings. I try hard to disregard it but pull my long black tunic tee shirt down to cover it.

"Who am I kidding?"

I am a full-on walking widow sanitary towel; nothing can cover this. People are fast. It's like I am in slow motion, and the people are on 1.5x speed or 2x if they are women under forty. I look at the women, studying them more than the salad bags I'm near. I see make-up and zip-up sweatshirt cardigans tied around waists, ponytails, hair washed, nails painted and iPhones in their hands, texting someone or other about the specials on Chicago Pizzas. Some have kids with them, and they look strange, somehow alien to me.

There are grandmothers too. Always near the baking section taking time to find a good deal on walnut pieces or those sweet sugared lemons for cake making. One of them smiles at me, and I can't return more than a curl of one side of my mouth. It looks more like a grimace, and I try hard to rectify it by saying something stupid like

"awwww huh-huh?"

As if she'd know, I was a grandmother, and I used to make cakes with grandkids and searched for good deals too. Once, when I was not dealing with death and dying, I did. She looks scared, and I'm begging her with my eyes to

"Notice me."

Yeah,

"*Now*, I want to be noticed?".

For her eyes to soften and recognise the dead husband in me. She doesn't, walks off, holding her bag and looks like she thinks I'm some deranged headcase, smiling and grimacing into thin air. Yes, all out of context. I could have explained.

I could have said what was happening. I could have told her and said,

"Look!"

holding out a book of vouchers, a pic of me in an apron and some dead husband slide show I carry in my bare hands. I could have followed her up the aisle and said,

"No! sorry love, look, I didn't mean to..."

And the God-like security guard would have made himself available, having already been following me. Because of my slow walking, in black, with shit hair, no make-up and hand movements at 0.75 x speed. My minimal food selection and zombie gazing at beans for ten minutes may also look like a drug addict shoplifter.

Yes, so she would have called him, and I'd then be crying and lost it and chucked out, and no one would know I was, in fact,

"A widow that needed compassion, a hug, some cake and a drink."

I needed a black tee shirt with the hashtag #WIDOW written on the front and #ThatsWhy on the back. I need the presentation I was giving in public to be made accountable for this

"Fucking huge experience that I wouldn't wish on my worst enemy."

For it to be understood before judgement came, when I passed someone, people in pairs, that saw me talking to him, crying or wiping up tears or just standing there,

"In trauma at a treacle tin."

to be understood. This walking madness to be given some mouthed and loving words as they huddle together, catching my look back at them. In their daily friendships, they have coffee in cafés and shop in supermarkets or at fruit and veg stalls. They would send the signal of all women rooting for other women:

"Oh, bless her...... but don't like her shoes much."

Sometimes Morrisons were the go-to place I could access online, but these sunglass days and long tunic tees were not nearly enough to cover me. I was safe in bed. I am lying in a bed with no clothing that looks like Instagram-ready pink fluffy Christmas fleece with hot chocolate and marshmallow toppings, with sunlight filter and pouty lip glossed lips.

········

Early Grief

I am lying in the fleece red and blue check pyjama bottoms he wore. The last set I bought him gave him the cool lounge look he had with blue slippers. The ones with good soles that he could still take the bins out in, that had pockets for guitar plectrums, bits of string and a radiator key.

These were washed, folded, and smoothed by hand on his clean white, fluffed pillow. There was a matching blue, thin cotton, V-neck pyjama top that I bought him in the hospital, which could easily be moved over his head after his operation. I grew to not like that even though it matched and would have been a good colour on Instagram if I were taking shots of my dead husbands' side of the bed for the world.

So readily, this got changed to the thin green one. This was vintage-styled and thin as fuck. And would be wet through when he came back from five-a-side football. Thin enough to be a good working tee when he was dabbling with the series three Land Rover on hot summer days. Or even at a blues gig coupled with his white blues hat with the brown trim. Authentically bluesy, vintage fonts and worked well for the long gigs he played.

Yes, this was his tee shirt. This was him. The him I wanted back in the bed, not the blue V-neck sick man, The healthy man with the oil of the engine under his fingernails still, even though he said,

"I *have* washed them."

That I'd complain about because of the tiny speck of satin that I saw once. The missing and aching. For a small oil spot, that I would've given anything for. Fuck the duvet, fuck the sheet. **His hands then were alive** and not a memory.

· · · • • • • · · ·

3rd Sept 2022 — Images of my death

I awake at 4 am after trying to sleep and playing on Facebook, and until I grew so tired, I dropped my phone on the floor. I put the phone on the bedside table on top of three or more poetry books I should be reading and pull the blankets over my arm.

I have my husband Dane's finger in my hand. The large index comfort finger to hold and scooch down into the pillow. The drift into sleep is ok, I'm not fighting it, and the smooth blackness under my eyelids begins to spread.

Within a minute, during the half-sleep state, where these images that often do arise, flashing their way onto my night-time storyboard, was a quick, not very well-paced, subliminal advert in the two-second image of a woman.

· · · • • • • · · ·

She is elderly, in a single hospital bed with a drip hanging to the right-hand side in a small but sunlit room. There are no people around her, and she looks like she is smiling, eyes closed and sleeping peacefully. I wonder who she is, looking at her small slim frame and dark shoulder-length and thinning hair. Her eyebrows are dark and thin, too and perfectly curved, framing her eyes as if formed from a fine white goat-haired Nara Fude. A master calligrapher's Japanese brush.

The lines in her skin are equally as fine and some deeper, across the bow of her lips. Her skin is light and yellow at the same time. Cadmium yellow mixed subtly with titanium white, there is the subtlest ultramarine tint of blue, shade thrown, from the window light, almost pearlised in the thin skin to the left side of her face and temple. There isn't any warm burnt sienna kissing her nose or cheeks or smoothed into the rice paper delicateness of her, but she wears a serene and contented face. I have painted her here for you in an appreciative but non-artist way.

I fear I am clumsy with a brush and have a deep need to hold one, but fail, even on make-up. I am reminded of how much I fail, but my attempt to paint comes flooding back right here and now.

·········

Painting with Bob Ross

Weeks before David's death, we watched painter Bob Ross on his YouTube channel, painting quickly, and we tried to follow suit. The arts and crafts acrylic painting that I promised I would do, and strewn around pastels and charcoals, were taken out of cupboards and presented to David in our now *artists'* front room with hand-held Amazon 9x10 canvas squares.

I painted along to a Bob Ross winter scene, and David created his own. A heart-breaking 'dark sunset.' The brushes were the grandkids, two for him and a stressful search for others until *I* found two. A lipstick one and a grabbed orange record player fanned brush. I use this to accentuate the leaves on the tall, thin winter trees I saw on the TV screen.

That was the first time I'd ever painted with or without David in ten years.

·· • • • • • • ··

On the next hospice day visit with him, I would bring my iPad and paint with a room full of others watching Bob Ross in *their* art room. I explained that Bob Ross was

"This cool white American dude with a fabulous Afro and says, **right-on** a hell of a lot."

They all laughed, and we painted. He was showing us the 1970's palette of his soul, and I was punctuating the heartache I held of everyone's soon-to-come deaths with the agreement that every time he said

"Right on..."

we would echo a

"Right on ..."

chorus back that we laughed at each and every time. I will be forever grateful that I didn't cry. These wonderful souls, comrades with cancer, were serene, at peace, graceful and gratefully painting their last.

·······

Images of my death continued..

Back to the room and the old woman with wonderfully painted brows that could have been painted by the Japanese Buddhist calligrapher she saw twice, a spirit guide seen before the Reiki she gave a client. Yes, these images and vision offerings are as vivid and as detailed as this woman's face. The realisation came slowly that she was me in many years to come. I am alone, with no husband by my side and no children near me, yet I look content. In a soft and peaceful light, I may be sick and recovering or have passed. I ponder this for a moment and assume this was a message for me to see. I feel no fear of any death and am reassured that the afterlife will be one of peace.

Chapter Twenty

Dad Dream - A Visit - Zoom - Angry at God and a Goodbye

Dad Dream – Visit - 27th Sept – 2022

I woke from a dream crying tears that told me I didn't know what had happened. My husband Dane comes to hold me, and I fall into his arms with the catch breath retelling of the tale and tears. Tears grow in weight inside my eyes and heart and fall like sandbags bombed onto the covers below me.

·· · · •· • · · · ·

Zoom

"We were in a Zoom, and my Dad, he's going to die, Dane! He was speaking and said, "You know Trish, I can't do something (illegible) anymore." That's when we both look off Zoom camera at each other, and I do a 'we're *going*' thumb, and you nod back in reply. You could hear and see that he didn't have long, and me too, an...an... an' I knew we were getting up to leave, soon as this Zoom call was finished an... an... and you'd be driving me there!"

He held me closer as the tears were streaming down my face and the realisation slowly fell into my resistant- daughter-mind that

"Dad *was* dead!"

He was *not* imminently dying ... we were *not* going on a fast drive across London to get to him, and we *didn't* live in London. We were, in fact, in another country altogether. I am catching the smaller snotty drips in my hand and bawling now, sitting upright in the bed.

"I'll get you some tissue."

he says and comes back with it in time to catch the second round of Blitz bomb tears that are hurtling like trapezing, kamikaze pilots, parachute-less from the Pain-Plane splashing on the blue-grey cobbled streets of my childhood home in London, Stepney. These wet fireworks explode.

They are full of confetti memories, birthday parties and Spanish music. Close-ups of his Mariachi thumb, football pools, score draws, olive oil in my earache-ear, Johnny Cakes, bakes, cricket snoozing, and Formula 1 lullabies heard on a sofa beside him.

·· • • •• • • • ··

My husband joins my tears with his as he realises I now know that

"My father *is* dead."

and that the Zoom view we just had, was him coming to see me, to say

"Hello"

to my 'alive husband' and to say

"He heard me read."

what I'd written at the poetry Zoom earlier. The excerpt on Family Grief and his death. So, this was him coming to offer that he

"Was there, listening."

and being with us and that, in this dream visit, he'd painted a different picture for me. Where I was *with* a husband that *could* drive me to see him before he died in the hospital.

·· • • • •• • ··

A Visit

As stressful as it was, I had to visit my dying Dad, staying in a hotel with my soon-to-die and cognitively impaired brain-tumour-ravaged husband, who got ill and had ambulances called for *him* too in the middle of the night.

But we persevered, and both got to see my Dad in the hospital. My almost-dead husband said farewell to my almost-dead Dad, and then I took him home and waited for the call.

·· • • •• • • • ··

It was a day later, and I insisted that I had David looked after by his brother. I left medication sheets and the medicine and told him all the food was already made and that I would be back very soon, and asked if he could please help this time because, if he didn't, I was actually walking out the door. He'd have to ring social services to get care for his brother as

"My dad is dying!!!!!!"

In a fit of exasperation and grief at the proximity of this death so very fucking close. David insists that this

"Will be ok."

and more or less forces his brother to take on this task. He finally does, and I thank my cognitively impaired, spot-on-husband. That knows,

"I'm at my fucking limit with doing everything alone" and knows I'm thinking,

"I'm so fucking, fuckin', fuckin' grateful you are still in there somewhere, and you can *still* see me for this one God damn minute!"

···•••••··

Angry at God

I turned to God, and anger from fuck knows where built, and I exploded my tirade inside into the inside-me-room I'm now in with Him.

"And yes, GOD" in this '*where-the-fuck-ARE-you* minute. Along with harder-than-hard Jesus. Gone to the pub? Fucked off? Cos, you and me? Well....."

(God is silent, a bit sheepish, but I continue)

"I seriously haven't got fucking time to talk with you right now. You and I know that I'll deal with it later, or You'll hear it later."

I still have reverence enough to put a flippin capital 'Y' in You.

"About, what *You* set before *me?* If I can't handle it, You'll ....put it before me? What the fuck is it? It's shit, is what it is. I can't handle anything right now. You fucking .... don't even...."

(God walks away to the side of the inside-me-room messing with some papers or shit).

"You gone silent? That's fucking right... Piece of fucking ....."

I want alcohol and ten cigarettes one after the other and to smoke them in angry

"Fuck off, why-they-gotta-die."

smoke! I sit on the arm of the sofa with my back to David. Exhausted, I breathe inside, fully. Exhaling out into the inside-me-room, where God tries to wander towards me, but I'm gone.

·········

A Goodbye

I get to Paddington Station, take a taxi to the hospital, almost falling out onto the street, and steady myself with my walking, now almost running stick. I'm being informed on my mobile by my family upstairs that he hasn't got long, and

"I still have the cheek, or whatever it is, to smoke one last cigarette?"

before I arrive in the dad-is-dying room. He is almost on the near rattle breath, and his wife, my step mum, is trying to feed him spoons of love and yoghurt. It dribbles down his chin along with her soon-to-be widow tears. We are there overnight, and the family share bonded grief and prayers around a bed. I come close to his ear to have this **one moment with him in *our inside-us-room,*** inside the dad-is-dying room I erect just for us.

I want to tell him all the things I couldn't say in the one minute I think I may have left with him before he stops hearing and can no longer feel the love in words uttered before the only sensation between us is touch before hands grow slowly cold in mine. I don't want his wife to hear these goodbye words that will spin her into **the *downward* I already live in**, that I know she is in, but I want to have some space in this very full room.

·········

My Goodbye

I make the structure of this father-daughter cocoon in a family of seven children, three he will soon reunite with and four, still five-year-olds or teens inside. Before the first sister's death took a little more away from him. He that remained after my mother left and two more children, now dead, pulling the last of a shroud around him, leaving him and us thread-bare.

·········

In the pieces of cotton that remain, I speak these words:

"Dad, you were the best father any child could want. You took such great care of us all. I am forever grateful you told me I was 'the jewel in your crown' in your speech at my wedding, and you are the best father anyone could want. You took care of us all and didn't put us into care when mum left, and you kept us together. I am so grateful.

I want you to know **everything you did was a lesson in love.** You taught us how to love children. You loved us all so much and your grandchildren. **You are so very loved.** We have all learned what loving a family has meant because of you.

We were all so proud to have gone to Trinidad to be with you that last time where you lived and to meet your family, our family. I was so grateful to have been there with you and proud to be your daughter. **To have sung with you**, you have your loving family all around you.

And **it's alright to go and be with family in spirit.** Your wife loves you dearly. **We will always love you.** You are my father, and I am your proud daughter."

··•··•••••··

I move away, still holding his hand and fearing other family members think

"I'm taking too much time."

I offer the little left back to them and his wife. I have said my goodbye. The following few hours are showered in prayers and gentle tears, and we are tired and watching the last of him slowly leave.

··•··•••••··

Death takes its time in these moments, and people are exhausted. Other family members indicate they will be

"back in the morning"

thinking

"death is going to be much later"

and they leave to go home, knowing that I and my brother and a niece are all with him and that we will

"call them if anything happens."

I don't have the heart to tell them;

"It *is* happening now"

They have hope, and I have a feeling. I prepare for a long bedside vigil and offer to get us food, coffee and anything to stay awake. I leave early to get to a local all-night shop and bring back cheese rolls, chocolate, coffee and cigarettes. I have no fear on the street as I usually do, as it feels like my aura is full of clear as fuck death and dying, and those that may cause harm to another will not mess with The Reaper companion I have walking beside me.

·········

The Reaper

The Reaper is selecting overpriced orange juice. The one that goes with soda bread and avocado, and I throw him a
"don't take the piss"
look.

He is twenty years of age, a cool dude that wears the latest Reaper designer threads and full-on Madonna Material Girl lyrics running around his head. His hair is slick, and his shoes are black crocodile skins. He's pretty cocky, bored and wants to get this job done. I'm sure he has an Instagram Reel to make with tips on how to be prepared, what to wear and what the latest Reaper Playlist should be when he turns up to *your* last party. I suffer him quietly. He watches me with bags of food and a tray of three takeaway coffees. And, no, doesn't help me carry any of this.

We get back to the hospital, and he's now disappeared.

·· • •• • •• ··

I bring food to my brother and niece and need to sit and eat. I look at my father's hands, looking like they're going blue, and I'm worried. My brother needs a cigarette, and we agree to swap vigil seats after I've eaten.

·· • •• • •• ··

The hospital lounge is an empty grey room with patient and visitor soft fabric seats and a coffee table. Its vast windows are peppered with London City lights twinkling, and I take this much-needed break.

I put the coffee and cheese roll onto the table, open the cling film wrap around the roll, and bring it to my mouth to take one bite. As I do, I see my Dad reflected in the huge city-lit window, well and healthy, with his dark Mario Lanza hair shining, and I immediately think,

"Wow, Dad! You look good."

Then, instantly remember that our loved ones in spirit always look good, their most glowing, young, healthiest selves, in their best and coolest clothes. I then put the roll down as I realise he is about to die. I think almost out loud,

"Oh no, for fucks sake, not right this minute. I'm so hungry."

I'm half hoping he hasn't heard me in this final below-my-breath disrespect. He speaks:

"I'm going now, Trish."

He turns to 'walk' into the city lights both behind and in front of the window. Both in and outside the room.

"Dad, one minute,"

I say, with the very guilt I *should* be feeling,

"Not yet."

My bargaining lasts for approximately five seconds, then I get up and rush back into the dad-is-dying room and phew, he is still with us. I know not for long and that this *leaving the body in his spirit* will come to me in these ways before the final breath is drawn. I know this. Yes, I know this. More than anything, I know this as it had already happened to me before.

· · • • • • • • · ·

When my mum was soon to die, waking me from a dream in the nearby hospital hotel when I'd finished my thirty-three-hour bedside 'shift.' I awoke within minutes of laying my head on the pillow, dreaming of two seven-foot must-be-angels, holding her under her arms, oil put on her head, and her saying to them sadly,

"So, do I have to go now?"

I awoke and sat bolt upright, texted my sister this 'spiritual truth' and rushed back to the hospital to the bedside vigil for her. My brother and sister confirmed she had just been given Catholic prayers from the priest and had the Last Rites, and *they* were on either side of her holding her under her armpits. So, I had recognised it all before. She looked good in that too, cheeky in fact and her hair, bottle dye and Irish auburn and still very beautiful. So, we get to look our best in these last visitations.

·······

Dad looked like he was thirty-five, slim and healthy, ready to dance with people and sing his once kitchen arias on a film set in lights to a welcoming female 1950s cinema-loving crowd.

·······

I am back holding his hand and try to tell my brother, but he, like me earlier, needs a cigarette, and we swap vigil seats. I worry about calling people, and we discuss it for a while until it's clear a call has to be made, and we begin ringing around. I don't recall when he finally went, maybe sometime around

5.30 am, but I feel he had already left the body in spirit. I shared prayers again over Dad's body and for my siblings and family's comfort.

I am silent, quiet, and not angry at the young and equally well-groomed crafty Reaper, as I say,

"Probably rushing back for his next Instagram Reel."

Yes, crafty slipping into the dad-was-dying room soon as I took a break. So, I am in total acceptance, and this matter happened quickly. I am aware of Kubler Ross now, and this acceptance comes quick. I have no fight left in me, no hurt, just the rush back to my soon-to-be dying husband and the soon-to-be widowland I am building for myself at home.

·········

Zoom continued...

So that was Dad, and we were back on the bed, me still crying softly and saying 'Dad came back' to say he heard me at the Zoom Open mic, where I'd read the 'Family Grief' excerpt and was showing me he was there earlier tonight. He heard me and knows my *alive husband. And* that I wanted to be with my soon-to-be dying husband at his death. He knew I needed my husband by my side on that final visit. He was saying that

"*This* husband would have been able to take you, but David wasn't. David had said his goodbye to him and returning again would probably have been far too much for him."

That Dad was saying to me,

"*You* were the one that had to come, and yes, *you* needed a strong husband with you, for *you*, but this was never feasible, and that's alright. I know your wishful thinking of where you are now in your life and your alive husband meeting me is also not possible, so I have placed this dream for you on the table between two worlds on the cloth near a candle in our hearts and minds and in our spirit of connection that will never cease."

And finally,

"I like him; he supports you, and you are my daughter and never alone."

Chapter Twenty-One

Widow Support

The widows' support groups online were plentiful. One I joined was the Bereaved by a Brain Tumour Facebook Group. These were the most incredibly supportive places. We had online help and were there for each other on WhatsApp or Facebook Messenger or calls at silly-o-'clock in the

"don't worry, I'm awake."

crisis line.

Online support for first days widows, shopping at a supermarket, meeting family after funerals or discussing what to do with a family who had other ideas about the ashes, were the most terribly supportive places. Sometimes filled with accounts of how we all managed work, or a walk, or a talk with 'the normals' (those that haven't experienced this loss and widow madness trauma). There was another group, Widows drinking wine or something. It was great at first, we were able to be ourselves without worrying about Facebook group penalties for the odd swear word.. and clearly, with my angry that he died, potty mouth, I would fit in... this was good to let loose on the pain. Really good and much spent with the sentiment of

"Can't wait to get home."

From work or choir or wherever, and maybe open a bottle of wine. I had Jack Daniels and coke, and I knew this was a group of comfort, but I slowly left having moved more and more into my Reiki, and therapy as a I had a telephone counselling offer and of course, my healing music. I also noted I was using less ice cream, cake and never being a big drinker, alcohol too. It was becoming healthier grief. I was wanting my authenticity in grief. All feelings felt.

·········

Jackie - A Widow's Neighbour

My new neighbour introduced herself to me and knew of my husband's death. Her twenty-something son had stayed in the house she'd bought next door before she moved in when he moved further into the city. He was often great musical support to my husband, playing blues guitar alongside him and me, feeling like they were just men in a room with two guitars whilst I took five minutes of respite in the kitchen.

It was a warm connection, and my husband and I were glad of this. He would have a chance to share some more of his blues riffs as if a legacy to the young. I was so grateful for this young man; his empathy and understanding were terrific and very appreciated.

·· • • • • • • • • ··

Jackie, his mum, was widowed and shared her story and condolences. I explained how important her son was to my husband and of the music and care he'd shown and that she should be so very proud, as this kind of care and understanding was exceptional.

It was not long before the daily tears I'd shed were noticed, on doorsteps, through walls, and at differing times of the day and night. Most mornings, when I stood in the same unwashed dressing gown, smoking and looking heavenward, she would ask how I was. This checking in with me, this level of understanding and my reply were nearly always the same.

"Yeah, I'm getting there."

And then I'd continue with some morsel of what I thought was neighbour-widow truth, half-truth, not wanting to offend, wanting all of me to be readily fixed and able to say

"Lovely weather today!"

The things I wanted to say in the future, The future I wasn't yet in. The reality was that I didn't give a shit about the weather or anything. I would stand in all weathers with this one unwashed fuck-sake dressing gown, again with the no knickers, and keep trying to tie a cord around the belly of grief that was howling inside. This Irish mum memory is fully present in her advising,

"Fix up. Da neighbours!"

I'd get mum off my back with,

"I haven't worn knickers for a week, and I've tied the belt cord FFS."

Mum would be silent as my neighbour, in her kindness, approached.

"I'm going to Morrisons if you want anything"

Offered as if she had full knowledge that my feet don't work like they used to, now that he's dead.

"Oh, thank you, yes, if that's alright. A pint of milk and some bread?"

I needed so much more.

Here is an accurate list:

1. Can't be bothered - microwave meals x 10
2. Toilet rolls
3. Mansize tissues

4. Some black leggings x 5 from Primark

5. Maltesers – Biggest Box - x 4

6. Packet noodles x 20

7. Haagen Dazs ice cream - 20 gallons

8. Jack Daniels and coke x 4 bottles of each

9. Butter

10. A huge cake for any time I cry

11. Ham

12. Peanut butter x 5 gallons

13. Jam x 5 gallons

14. Essential oil x 35

15. Some pretty shit for looking at in a trance

16. Sellotape for I don't know why

17. Envelopes for I don't know why

18. One carrot – for I don't know when

19. Anything that is warm, easy to heat up, not crunchy in my mouth, or too hard to swallow. (probably macaroni cheese)

20. and 5000 x tea light candles.

So, I just asked for milk and bread, and she'd pop back with our arranged plan.

"Yeah, leave it on the doorstep,"

The

"Because I might be busy crying."

Over the coming days, weeks and months, she was there for so many things. Shopping at Morrisons grew as a regular offer, and my feet and broken widow legs were grateful. Followed by trips to Sue Ryder Hospice Charity Shop to help me get rid of things as and when I could touch things. Again, sitting with me and listening to the whole widow outage for that week, the loud tears, or the loud reiki music.

Or even the rock choir songs, our between-walls text message song requests, and the birthday party held at her garden with neighbours she'd arranged when I spent a widowed birthday alone during the pandemic Lockdown. The numerous, steadying of my nerves with that lovely French drink, which was a special treat she gave herself after holidays in France that she chose to share with me. Or the summertime fruit ciders in the hot sun when she coaxed me. Or collecting me when I'd collapse in tears inside supermarkets when I was grief frozen at bus stops or simply in town.

The grandchildren she shared with me that I was grateful for, and their warm acceptance of me, and a lyrical toddler and his older sister's purest angelic Scottish voices calling my name,

"Tish?... Tish?"

Pulling me into a world I should be living in.

Or the letters she helped me to read because my brain was full of widow cells and fog. The support that I needed when she'd heard me crying about some shit or other that had happened with family, and forever unspoken recognition of my constantly wanting out of the pain. And the pain, and the pain and the ever widow pain.

··········

We sing keep-it-together karaoke on the PA through walls, her select numbers from rock and pop bands like Queen. Wet Wet Wet txt-messaged to me, or other upbeat songs that help to keep the widow wolf pain at bay, or we meet, in two-meter distancing in gardens, on summer days, talk over my ironing board, filled with letters whilst I'm now drunk and crying cos
   "my husband is still flippin dead."
   Still, we'd had widow fun on a wet summer's day with even newer neighbours, now embroiled in the Saving a Widow Film, screened right in front of their eyes. After snotty tears and
   "Someone Like You"
   Adele, at rock gig decibels, swaying back and forth through my microphone comfort, drunk hugs with widows and wives and, oh, so many
   "Just gonna sleep now'
   apologies.

··········

And she was there too when I was 'saved' by the vicar from the Reiki in the exorcism performed, and I instantly became a Sorry-Again-Christian, ready to give up everything that kept me sane to enter into prayerful service. And, whilst the church may have felt this Reiki was a bit rubbish for my despairing widow heart. And that it might be made better with cake, tea and my healing prayer hands used for others under their tutelage; my widow neighbour shook me out of the stupor I was in and said,

"No, Tish! That's been the making of you. You love your Reiki."

And I was deradicalized all at once. She saved me on calls, in messages, and in the following year with the pull myself together of a widow relationship gone bad. She read my poems and excerpts from this book and demanded

"More comedy!"

and I agreed. She regaled with others in my joy at returning to music. Was happy that I was singing again, for me, for others and with others in the choirs. She listened to family worries, was always supportive, and encouraged me to

"Get on the plane!"

to meet my new online widow-poet love in San Francisco. Whom I then married.

She has been amazing and still looks out for me, helps me with my home, and was the strength I never had and hoped would grow inside me. I was a widow watching her widow-land with hope for me in mine.

· · · • • · • • • · ·

3rd Nov 2022 - 2.30am

I wrote my new website newsletter, had a break for a ciggie, came out of the bathroom and heard a TV ad on.

The YouTube singing bowls I write and sleep with are audibly and loudly cut into with the words

"I'll be looking out for you in San Francisco."

I say,

"Thanks, Dave."

Chapter Twenty-Two

The Five Stages of Grief and Me

G rief is a complicated and potent emotion; sadly, we may all probably meet grief and likely go through it at some point in our lives unless we are unconnected to anyone and do not expect it soon. If you don't have family, parents, grandparents, or friends, there is likely a state of grieving at some point. There are different theories about how we process our grief.

I've used the Kubler-Ross five-stage theory, and I'll add a few of hers a bit later. Still, the stages of grief are thought to be the same for each person. Some people can go from one stage to another in a linear fashion and do so in a 'timely' manner. Some might even hurdle a stage quickly or may even skip a stage, depending on their circumstances.

Others may get stuck on a single stage of grief and might find it difficult to move on or through to the next stage. However, knowing there are stages may help you understand where you're at in understanding your emotions.

It's also good to be able to do an 'oil check' assessment of how well you are progressing through them and 'monitor the tyres' for the grief journey you're about to take. It helps to know what this new shit is because it is shit. Shite, in fact.

To get OK with shite being a part of your new life. Accept that only you are responsible for cleaning it up, out and away from the grief home you live in because that's where you will be, and you have to make a new life with healthy grief.

The mind has built-in protectors and allows us to bear the unbearable, and I know that this grief will feel like it is flippin unbearable. But we are here, I am here, you're still here, reading this book and watching my trauma shower of shite get sorted, and if you're grieving, you will too. We are resilient and can cope with vast amounts of shite in the world. We are innately survivors of shite, war, abuse, or trauma, and we inherently want to remain such.

These five stages of grief may make you feel like it doesn't precisely fit where you are and who you are at any given time; that's OK too. You may not see yourself exactly in the Kubler Ross five stages theory, precisely how it's mapped out, but that doesn't matter. We are all individuals and are more than any written theory. We all know one thing, though. We've all got this new thing to deal with. We know that, like other people, we want to regain our lives and stable footing. We all have a right to retrieve ourselves and our lives from the mountain climb that grief is.

We're supposed to go *through* these stages, process how we are, move into a healthy acceptance of the loss, and start our lives again. So, bearing in mind I did not follow these in any linear fashion, I will share them below. I will argue with these, too, haha, along the way as well.

·········

Denial –

The first stage of grief is denial (sometimes shock and denial). Hearing of someone's death, it may take a moment to process what we actually hear, especially if the death was unexpected. The news of a devastating loss can leave us frozen in disbelief, and denial may follow. People do these things before sharing the information, like

"Are you sitting down?"

possibly for fear of the listener fainting or having their knees buckle from under them.

When my mother was told of the first death of three young adult children, she went straight into denial - such was the shock, and denial was the first response.

"No, no, no!!!!! I was only talking to her last week."

The mind simply protected her from the devastating news. She couldn't process this news, which was simply unacceptable. A numbness may follow, and a gentleness will be well afforded by those around the griever. Numbness is your body and mind's way of taking care of you, letting you only deal with what you can handle, which may be simply small amounts of information. It's nature's way of letting you deal only with your emotions that you can handle.

Look at it like a duvet protecting your mind and emotions from feeling the whip-ass cold of grief in its full wild wet, and stormy sea that you may now be swimming in. The most important thing is navigating these waters and finding the shore. Shipwrecked or not, you will have to reach that shore and gather yourself for the onward and painful grief journey.

·· • • • • • • • ··

Anger –

This stage of grief is possibly the most heart-wrenching, exhausting and painful. There can be all kinds of anger. Anger at doctors, God, and the universe, and lashing out verbally at family, friends and even work colleagues. Even if this death was expected, this stage can be exhausting and leave you full of self-reproach. If in the case of a terminal illness, the death of a loved one is looming, there may be something called **pre-emptive grief**, and here all of the five stages play their part too. This was precisely where I was, knowing my husband had a terminal illness and the aggressive and incurable brain tumour had a prognosis of dying between four and thirteen months. I was in denial immediately. I said,

"Come again?"

and followed the doctors outside to ensure I heard what I had heard. Then I had to immediately process this and make sure I accepted this. I asked them to repeat this to me again and again for the two minutes I was outside his room. I saw their pain on how to share again and again and why I needed it repeated. They were gentle, and they understood what I was doing. I knew that by doing this, there was no way I was going to deny this.

It was my way of fortifying myself and not hiding this from my mind so that I could verify that he understood what was said to him too. I could and would then gently tell my husband what I knew if he didn't.

As a carer for my husband, cognitively impaired and needing 24-hour supervision, I had little time or space to be angry.

His well-being was the top priority. I was also angry again about not having the chance to express anger anywhere.

After his death, I wasn't angry immediately. Still, I dealt with the things that needed to be done - actually, I was mad at my walking stick for not being strong enough for him to be able to die at home, but I wanted this last moment not to be filled with anything other than my husband feeling my love and for his last days to be gentle and completely full of care.

This allowed us to just be husband and wife and to say goodbye. My anger afterwards kicked in around three weeks when I first put pen to paper. I was devastated and angry at my husband.

"You said you'd always be here."

crying and typing - he had

"Flippin left me"

We were supposed to be married until we both died. I kind of thought that meant together at eighty or something. But just because that's what I wanted didn't mean that would happen.

Anger was then thrown around liberally at family members, particularly my daughter. Yep, the closest to you will get it. I'd write it and notice it in verses in my first grief poem:

This day, a child soon to wed,

has lost her mum at a hospice bed...'

Then in a further verse:

'But this day took much away from me,

In rooms, I watch life falter,

I have a widow tongue in me,

Now fear losing of the daughter.'

The entire poem gives a good breakdown of the grief and 'tearing out hair', utter pain I was in, and my account of how much I was in the, right up to my forehead, Anger stage.

·········

Bargaining –

Bargaining didn't feature in me much with the outside world. Before my husband's death, yes, with anyone that could save him. Doctors, Holistic therapies, alternative therapies, praying to God, organic teas, foods, Neurosurgeons, International Brain Tumour conferences, newspapers, medical research, and the begging of the public to help me do that research.

There was the ongoing search for a cure, encompassing the world of knowledge of brain tumours, angiogenesis and trident therapies that may halt progress. Finding out about Essiac tea, a Native American herbal tea that had helped many people with cancer, and the vitamins, antioxidants and physical strength needed to do all of this.

This was my pre-emptive bargaining. If I had strength, regardless of my on-it-for-ten-years walking stick and being absolutely exhausted, I knew I would give my husband a shot at a longer life. Maybe a cure in my disbelief at doctors, and more importantly, my husband thought I could. He'd said so to a newspaper journalist, so I had to show him I had

"tried, tried, tried."

I was bargaining with all of the above, hoping I might be at least honourable as his wife. In his expectations of me, he would know that I did and

"Gave my everything."

Only until he accepted that this was not going to work did I allow myself and him into the acceptance of his impending death. At least, this would be the gentle, reiki, blues music, loving and accepting death it would become.

·········

Pain –

This is not one of the five stages - but I need it to be here as it was definitely my experience. I was in pain as soon as I called the first ambulance when the paramedic on the phone said,

"Can he lift his arms?"

I immediately felt shot through the stomach by those words, knowing fully that if he couldn't turn the key in the ignition of his car and asked me to call an ambulance, this was 'stroke serious' at least.

You've read earlier in the book just how absolutely painful this has been for me and have suffered the reading of that pain, the step by step, walk with me in this pain that I've made you do. I've planted you into this forced listener role in the warm and comfortable seat you're in or the bed you are duvet wrapped in, maybe in your own pain and grief.

Or perhaps you are with a husband, lifelong partner, or some significant other that is holding your feet at the end of a sofa.

First, let me say I'm sorry you are now captive, and maybe this is a good time to get a hot chocolate or something or get a fresh cup of tea or coffee. Or maybe, perhaps, this is a good time to stop and take a well-being check. I'm hoping you are doing that along the way because

"This is where I fucking scream, analyse and scream again, and say sorry and feel guilty."

and all kinds of stuff.

I'm even going to have to stop *myself* for well-being checks. This is a rollercoaster, and I apologise for this bat-shit crazy pain you're about to read. I won't come up for breath unless I have to, but here goes.

Trigger warning: child/mother traumatic death.

Imagine a child at your breast or watching your child's mother nursing, and at that most beautiful and loving moment in your life, an earthquake hits, and the roof falls on top of you. There is no getting them out, and all are utterly lost, and I mean all. You are in the remains of a life that has crashed down around you, and they are gone. Searing pain – searing like a steel girder that struck you in your abdomen, and you feel you may very well die too.

Trigger warning – Extreme Infidelity / Homelessness / Tsunami

Imagine a husband or wife that sleeps with your best friend, that says
"Sorry..."
that you then forgive and then proceeds to do this all over again with your three other remaining best friends, leaving you now with no friends, no trust and that same steel girder struck through your abdomen. The final blow is that they have thrown you out to move their latest conquest into your home and marital bed and take care of your children, which you now have no family access to, and some legal advisor says

"There's nothing they can do."

Then imagine that there was another earthquake, and the street you now have to live on is being poorly evacuated, and a Tsunami is coming, and you might die too.

Trigger warning – Disney Wicked Witch / Killing Snow White

Now, imagine a mother with evil powers like the Wicked Witch Stepmother in Snow White. Who approaches you with arms outstretched but magically puts both her hands inside your chest and pulls out your pumping heart when you thought she was just coming to hug you.

And finally, imagine a husband that had skin-to-skin contact with you every day. That held your feet, rubbed your bad knee, made love to you. Kissed you, took the bins out and laughed at your bad jokes. Calmed you by rubbing your bum, stopped you smoking for two years by rubbing your bum, or simply rubbed your bum. Who was ever faithful, smiled every day, did karaoke with you. Bought you everything you ever wanted, a dressing table, bread machine, coffee machine, sewing machine, an Angela Lansbury Murder She Wrote bike and a drum kit.

········

Now imagine there being an earthquake and all of the people above were there, and you couldn't do anything to save them. Imagine also, War-torn Syria, famine in Ethiopia, Hiroshima, and all war-torn and hungered countries. And you're in a room, and those people and those images are all around you.

Every day for a month or four, or eight or more. You feel tears and cannot do anything about that but sit in the rubble of those emotional earthquakes, shock, horror and loss. Add to this the tears that Jesus had, The Prophets, or Princess Diana for everyone, or your family watching each siblings' death and their parents' grief and deaths.

Add these things to the debris you are now in. Look from the edge of a safe part of that room, maybe on a doorstep, or threshold of the patio, look into the windows of patio doors still just about intact and offer something to that person in the middle. That person you are looking in on or who *is* you.

·····•·•····

The tears will also fall like rain. Some fast, some like a daily drizzle with dry bits, some full-on torrential, some clearing the mud, clogging up a drain cover, only to be filled with leaves and debris again. I'm sure if you are watching and still with me and haven't spilt your coffee and shot up to get a cloth, that here is where your tears are given, like gently tossed tiny coins in a fountain of hope because there are no words that can account for the tragedy of all or any of the above.

And I want to let you know that each tiny coin of empathy you throw will be gathered and are the stepping stone out of this desolation. Suppose you are on the edge of those patio doors, or near the fountain or even closer than that and feel able to reach out a hand.

In that case, this one act will bring that person, at least on the edge of the fountain, to sit and gather for a while, to look back at what just happened and to move with hope into the next stage of grief.

·········

Depression –

There is a way of being that people call depression that is both an unusual fit and atypical in the signs shown. Kubler Ross may have looked at this primarily from the perspective of those dying. As opposed to the griever, this is liberally applied to the bereaved, and I hold a differing take on it.

This stage, she felt, was a time of being in full awareness of one's own death and feeling that in its entirety. This stage would last for a while, and in the case of her hospice work, would clearly be for a limited period until they reached acceptance and finally died. How long would that 'limited period' be, I don't know. But, in the case of those newly bereaved or not and specifically in my Widowland, I've found myself in, it may generally last forever, in deeper and lesser degrees.

What? I hear you say. Forever? Yes, my dear friend.

Let's first look at what we might all think the definition of depression is. Feeling extremely sad, not doing what you usually do (did if you look back as a non-widow) over at least a couple of weeks, a month even and unable to return from that without help. Whether a therapist or some intervention, clinical or through family and friends.

Yep, that's a bit simplistic. And, there will, of course, be the additional psychosomatic effects of pain held in the body; for me, these were: heartache, felt as what feels like heart attacks, emanating from the centre area of my chest, all the way through the back and deepening each time I cried the 'big tears', and were the headaches probably. Through the crying, but sometimes just there a hell of a lot.

General pains across my head, all around my head, migraine feeling probably. Heavy legs, heavy as fuck, can't walk sometimes. Then shooting pains from one end of my body to the other, possibly fibromyalgia in type. Tummy troubles, from the gut-wrenching, good old anxiety attacks from trying to get out of the house. Or having an awareness of

"'He's dead!'"

come slap me in the face, womb things, again sharp pains or 'not filled with his baby' pains, and arms that only go so high (waist high) held tight into the body, and only managing to put plates back on the first shelf as reaching higher made me cry.

· · · • • · • • · · ·

The assessment of depression, whether in person or in a phone call, might have the assessor ask about the things you did before.

"Are you able to do the things you enjoyed before?"

But your answer may bring up all the memories of a life shared.

And those things you did together are brought to your mind in your reply. The images of who you were come flooding back.

"I enjoyed cooking big lasagnes,"

and thinking,

"I can see the bubbling cheese topping,"

and the edge of my apron as I bend down and

"I can feel the weight of it,"

as I banged the oven tray on top of the stove because

"I was near to dropping it."

And

"I remember the smell,"

and would think,

"I know he loves this smell,"

And I know he's looking forward to this. Remembering him playing the guitar still and watching the TV news with the sound down. And then suddenly recalling,

"Ooooh, I've got time for one ciggie,"

on the doorstep, and the glass of

"Champagne, he poured for me,"

hopeful of some tipsy wife action later. And recalling how we watched TV together, and he'd ask for

"Ice cream, thanks."

and I'd get it, and he'd rub my feet, But you simply answer (vocally),

"No, I don't do lasagnes anymore."

And you might start crying at this point, but the assessor, with their tick boxes, is moving on, and you aren't following because this memory has grabbed you. You want to stay with the **lasagne** smells and all the smells you make in the oven on all the Christmases, and then you are like an automaton in your answers, and you have lost her train of thought, and she has lost you like you lost them and your outside world seems so far away. The one in this room or on this call. Because it is – and you are an observer of the life you had before and watching the 'happy' you had before, and all you remember is much more smiling in your life.

And then, all the memories are there, each one entering your consciousness fast, like a Viewmaster slide show toy, that you click, showing pictures of Karaoke nights, parties, laughing as you have to wee in a bush on a night out, after too much cider on the walk home.

"You see his willy,"

and the red sarong thingy he loved, and you momentarily wonder if

"Any other willy?"

or

"Maybe a woman?"

because you

"Can't imagine other willy?"

And

"Women would just hug, wouldn't they?

Then another tear falls, and you're back clicking the Viewmaster, now showing you passing him

"Yeah, the screwdriver."

Or a cup of tea, or arguing about whether something is

"A wrench or a spanner"

and he

"Should have been clearer,"

and of your own tool kit he bought you to stop you med-
dling with his, and dribbling curried chicken at your dads'
house, and passing a serviette, and the feel of the serviette on
his beard, and him feeling annoyed and mothered by you, but
still likes it, this man-boy, and him reading to grandkids from
story books and his big belly they squished up against and
loved, and the sand at Cornwall, and the wind, and the funny
time he zipped himself into the wet suit the wrong way round,
and the running towards the waves and the teenage grandson
when he was five, that squealed,

"This is the best time of my life!"

as he held his little hand tight and ran back from the sea
with him, and the tears drop, and the images click each time
a tear falls, and the assessor or doctor or

"Whoever the fuck they are,"

is messing with this and these moments, and you're hostile
now because of that, but you don't show it, and they sound
caring, in some distant voice you can barely hear, but you
can't reach, you just can't reach that caring whatever it is,
because they are still the fuck, dead.

Exhale.....................................

So, this is where you get another cup of tea or something.
Damn it, and I'm going to have to stop and have a cigarette.

Here is some space. Take it. – (**Space – 2 x a day or as required**)

After The Space

OK. We good? I hope so. I'll continue.

Depression in grief is shown in the early snapshot, and the continuation of depression lessened and lessened as I learned how to cope with the loss. But it was always still felt.

It was in the pit of my stomach even when I wasn't crying my eyes out or just mooching through a hallway to make another fuck-sake dressing gown cup of tea.

There was always a 'can't be bothered to get dressed, especially as I was trying to work from home. I began getting out on a bike, to the choir, or walking and used these days to be focused on wearing something other than tucked-in pyjamas. I washed and showered and loved the hot water as it was again a comfort. And I'd try to get my hair done and some make-up on. In time, I would dress as if I wasn't widowed.

Slowly I became more able to enjoy clothes and even the momentary weight loss – yeah, about a year, and when the writing began and the poetry flowed, it was a way of dealing with the depression.

And clothes, poetry, and singing at the choir was more or less the only time I *wanted* to dress in clothes other than a widow pyjama wardrobe. Dressing gowns became my 'mother comfort'.

His pyjama bottoms were used too in the first year, just the bottoms. And then they were moved to the pillow as I found my own pyjamas, and they were soft and brighter colours than the black leggings and baggy anything tee-shirts. They were pink with black love hearts and were cheap as chips from Primark.

"But now, see, everything had to be soft as fuck."

including food, clothes, sounds, TV, news, and people. I was OK making my own noise and being sharp, widow sharp with everyone. I probably wasn't, but I knew I was irritated and aggravated at their non-blemished-ness.

I was **tarnished with death.** Tarnished, broken and less Doris Day or Julie Andrews about life.

"The hills are alive.....with other people's living huuus-bands."

So, yes, there was a whole new *depression me* that had been gestating for 13 months and born on his death. It lived. It breathed and growled at me, the washing up and everyone. It cried, howled, and dragged its bad leg behind it with the grief trap still attached. It cooked depression food.

·· · • · • · ··

Acceptance

Well, here we go, as this is the big one, and I'm going to have a ciggie for the biggie.

"How the fuck, does one accept?"

For example, that a 20-year marriage or a five-year marriage is over? That, the fuck-sake-someone you married walked out on you for a younger woman or man, hey, it all happens, and you've got to,

"get your big girl knickers on and suck this up."

This is hard-as-nails news for anyone. They make documentaries about this shit and TV shows to find out about this unacceptable shit.

So, suppose you think you could barely handle that. In that case, this will likely make you want to go on Jerry Springer or Rikki Lake and tell the world how you smash an imagined fuck-about husband's car windscreen with a cricket or baseball bat (please don't do that), but

"He didn't actually do that to *you*. He simply up and fuck-sake died."

Either way, he left you. ---- What I'm trying to say here is that there is no way this is easy, and like marriages that end, it sometimes isn't anyone's fault. Those guys just grew apart, and hey, life's a bitch, and then you die. So why not live and let die? Yup, I am full of old songs, huh? Live and *let* die? Let people die? Don't try to keep them alive when the sign says 'incurable'. Read the words again.

"In-flippin-curable."

And death is in-flippin-curable too.

So, we got to grow into our acceptance like the woman that got left. She'll kick and scream and want to let his tires down, snoop on his Facebook page, and compare herself to the

"Slut fuck he's buying shit for."

and

"She has wrinkles anyway! And look at the gap in her teeth."

She could punch the rest right down her throat! And she'll snoop less and less about what he's up to because a bunch of friends said,

"Come on, girl, get out and do yo' thang."

And she and you did do a little bit of yo' thang that they had to remind you that you still had. Slowly she and you start getting out and just being with the girls for a while, and in time she sees a nice picture of them both together with their kid smiling back at her, and

"Her teeth are *fine*, and she *doesn't* have wrinkles,"

and this is just about OK, to look at. And their kid looks happy, and his dad's making sure their kid got everything he wanted at school and for his 7th birthday, and they look fine. Someone said to come over for Christmas once, and she did, and now a year or so later, she and her are not exactly mates, but she accepts her and him and them all in this new stayed-together family. And she accepts he just fell out of love with her and moved the fuck on.

And

"*He* is still the fuck alive!"

and maybe she could have bargained with him and tried to win him back, maybe tried 'that thing' that he liked in bed, and even if she did or didn't, he should have, could have, stayed with her, but he didn't, and she's OK, now.....with that. And he would have

"At least been alive *for* her to *do* that.

·······

Acceptance in grief is knowing and understanding firstly that they died and aren't coming back, there's no winning or coaxing, there's no hoping, cooing or doing 'that thing', there is *nothing* you could have done or do to get them back.

Secondly, the acceptance of life in death. Yes, life in death. It's the awareness and ability to accept that life *is* just there to engage in and that you could, should and might carve yourself a new one. One made from the ashes, the rubble, or the crater you sit in.

Yes, you *will* find the crawl back up hard. Up there is a slip of sunlight coming up over the edge. The sunlight found in pictures of grandchildren born, which are being sent to you, that you look at with your husbands' candle-lit one. And you show these to him, and he says,

"Aww, he's beautiful."

You know that he's watching you and these pictures of babies or of you joining in at family gatherings smiling. And when you read stories to them on your own, and you imagine him stopping by the door to turn the light out, knowing you are almost there. And you turn a page and think you saw him, and you don't stop to talk to him. You just keep on reading.

Because *they* need you now, and they always did, but you couldn't reach *them* because *you* wanted to stay with *him.*

Even if you fought it. Even if you said you wanted to be with him eternal, you didn't **(I didn't)**, and you are here **(I am here)** because you accepted **(I accepted)** that death is a part of life, and Oh, my God...Lion King!

"The circle of ......"

Yeah, yeah, don't stop now! And as you read through to the last page of these story books, you are aware of the acceptance you are *now* having and that you are filling yourself with things and people, activities and love and light, and songs, family, friends, Facebook and food. And lastly, the acceptance of life in life.

Yes, more Lion King or Bedknobs and Broomsticks, and Angela Lansbury and cream tea and scones

"For a sixpence gor' blimey!"

Life is there – come and take a scoop! But this is not sofa ice creams, bed and dark chocolate Haggendaz – These are the technicolour raspberry ripple cones. The hundreds and thousands sprinkled on top, pinks and yellows stuck in your teeth, and hot chocolates with marshmallows and whipped cream days because *they and life* are fun. That wash it from your mouth word, spat up on death **can and will return.** And you'll have flashbacks to the darker Bournville days, but you'll wake up and light an incense stick one day and smile at the sunshine coming through a window. Not even baby pics. Wash up because you want to or

"Just for the hell of it."

Eat eggs with avocado on soda bread, poached with your teenage grandson and plan dinners and **your own huge lasagnes.** You may even find you want more as the sense of being alone and needing feet rubbed turns into

"Could do with a cuddle."

and maybe more. And you may or may not get more, and you may not be ready, or you may be, and this is all OK too. And if and when you do, or you don't, that will be OK too. Because you **accept yourself now, too, with your grief wounds.** And you'll remember him and cherish his memory and light candles and look at photos with more and more acceptance, and you; tell him how well you and the grandkids are doing, once in a while. And maybe he'll visit in a dream once in a while. And you'll be fine with that and maybe share that with your new widowed poetry man, and you'll both light candles for your dead husband and wife. And you'll still wear his ring, and like me, maybe get married again and not know what to do with his wedding ring. However, you wear it around your neck, still with yours and the engagement ring that you lost and found in the cat litter tray, and you'll share that pic on Facebook and all your friends that know your story will say,

"Oh, thank **God!**" or "**St Anthony!**"

Or just plain old

"Thank **Fuck!**"

And these are the acceptances you may face – the overall acceptance of death immediately, the ongoing acceptance of grief and the final acceptance of a new life, yours. Phew! Now let's put the kettle on.

Chapter Twenty-Three

Entering into Life

S o, I have left that section to the end because it wasn't what I thought at all during the being newly widowed or writing widowed days. Yes, I did think, what the hell is all this flippin stuff that I don't understand and am I going flip sake bonkers here. But just like we have to accept death is in-flippin-curable too, so too is life.

Life is in-flippin-curable every day, every single day. Whether we like it or not, the sun is going to shine, the rain is going to fall, and neighbours will bang on walls for the noise (not mine), and shoppers will knock their trolleys into your ankles, park their cars too flippin close to yours when you have bags and bags of crips for the teenagers.

And these teenagers will be just as sensitive, just as noisy, or flip sake loud as you were when you were a teenager, and vicars, will vic, employers will ploy, choirs will be on point or not.

And all over the world, babies will laugh or crawl. Kids and squirrels will try to make you happy with their smiles or cute attacks on you. And you will pull out bread for the birds or throw rubbish down a large wheelie bin and shout

"FFS"

to a teenager that emptied porridge in the bin bag. It's running down your washed dressing gown.. cos you did wash it, finally, and you did, get out and smile at the flip sake sun that did its conniving sunrise at you in the morning. Its' subtle, alluring sundown setting shit in the evenings. You were taken unawares and resisted, and

"You will, you will fucking-well, resist."

And you will find a way to trick yourself into that, being a safe place for you to be and get on all pseudo-happy and big girl knickers about your half-lived life. And you know, the funny thing about fuck-sake-life, is that she is one bitch that got your back. And then she will, yes, eventually, she will let you die too. Life, she flippin knows what you can and can't bear, will throw people and things your way, and you'll trip the fuck up and fall again. See that your dress is torn, but that don't matter because that's your raggedy tear. And people will see the raggedness and think,

"Aww, something happened to her."

and you'll say,

"Yeah, so, what? I'm this way because of it."

Or, on kinder days, you'll say

"It did. Thanks for noticing."

And then you'll sew that dress up, in time because of

"Your mum and da neighbours."

And

"At least you're wearing knickers now."

And at least the socks are now the same colour, and

"So, what if they aren't?"

Because nothing matters like it used to in your life, and you

"Give yourself a break."

and others will see that you are so much stronger and will give you a leg up. To get the fuck on or pass something your way, and you may or may not be interested, and that's ok too. And you'll be in the sweet shop of a new life, and you'll pick at cherry bombs and chocolate-covered honeycomb. And you'll think,

"Ah, my teeth, I want a whole set, stop eating that"

or doing that. And you'll want these teeth without fillings now to get you into the future or even a new one. And suppose you lost one like I have and

"The pirate gap!"

and the whole shebang, and your broken leg dragged behind you. In that case, you'll bandage up and take it to the pub with you and tell your story over a pint of cider or prosecco to another young widow that is new to the Costa-Del-Shite, and she'll be listening and thinking how wise you are and how

"You got through this shit fest."

And she'll say,

"Thank you."

And at night, you'll think of her in her own bed, crying her eyes out and you'll say to the Universe,

"For fucks sake, another?"

And you'll know you can't stop that pain from happening, but you are sending her love, even if you don't know her, and you'll be open to the possibility of loving complete strangers in this way, because that is what it is. And life is flippin well going on and on, and you are part of it, and you are helping yourself and others, and when you can't, you hang back and know they will be alright because YOU were and ARE alright.

And I'm telling you here and now, that you may cook, or not, you may sing, or not, in this re-entering life again, you may meet a man, fall in love again, or not right now, as it might also be too soon, and you may falter and get back up and find another and get married or not, you may write a book like I did and tell that story, about that new thing you did and call it The San Francisco Story' and fly to another country or feel like you're in Timbuck-Flippin-Tu or not, and have a new life or not, and all along the while you will still be loving the one that died, and feel the loss, but the moment you think its all too much you'll find another friend, or a message you wrote yourself stuck on a mirror or at the back of your dressing table drawer that said,

"Go girl, "

or

"Tish got her thang'

or think,

"Tish got it back"

or broken or half broke but it was and still is *your thang* and no one can take that away from you. Your experience that you will learn from, just like you did and do in the grief you,

"Swam-the-fuck in."

and rested on banks from and at the end of this swimming pool of tears, you'll bob up and down, get your shoulders in and out of the water and put those stupid goggles back on and swim your fucked up, front crawl, back to another shore. Twenty times even.

And that's enough cos

"You're not fat, you're not fucking fat,"

and

"Yes, you are a little bit."

but you're not doing the Olympics, and it's a long slow swim, but there are towels at the end when you pull yourself up, and out of that water. And they are white and fluffy or even the big one with the hole in when it got caught on the radiator. And you still use it because it's yours. And it's the favourite one you remember you got favourites of this and that of anything. And you'll start using them and using

"The blue velvet dress for Christmas,"

and glittery stuff in eye shadows or lipsticks, and

"You'll look alright. You'll look nice again."

And feel nice again, and no one is stopping you now because you are using this experience to tell you that is exactly what life is about. The pain of death and the Lion King thingy wot not, and you know what I mean, and then,

"Sister of sweet pain and misery."

then you'll be thinking

"It was a learning"

that no one ever told you, you had to learn,

"But you did!"

and it was a process of doing one exam in school. Call it a mock exam, say when you are kicking feet under a desk, chewing bubble gum and flicking paper at your other friends because you were

"That kinda girl."

but you

"Knuckled down when you had to, yeah? Yeah, you did."

And this was the learning and growing you had to do, to be prepared for the other deaths that will come and the life that you got stronger from, and now, the day is yours to get ice cream in or not, to allow health and talking and sunshine into your day. And

"Open the fucking curtains"

or blinds and

"Tidy the shit up"

around you because you are worth not sitting in shit, sister. You are worth living in life. No matter what you carve out for yourself, it is yours. And finally. You will tell them,

"I did it, babes, I did it."

or even

"I'm doing it! I'm doing it!"

And they will say to you,

"Yeah, you are. Now go on, girl."

Or

"Go on wid ya,"

like me mudder would say, or

"Yes, darling I'm watching you. We are watching you, we got your back."

And you know that, You got your back, and you will be like,

"Aww thanks'

as if you are just dropping them a quick Whatsapp message or a postcard from the life of Make it Again, and

"You're too busy to talk,"

to them, and won't feel guilty because

"This is important."

And you and they want you to engage in life, and now you will let their spiritual calls go to the answerphone, and that'll be alright. And you'll update them when you can and say,

"Happy New Year"

and

"Happy Christmas,"

and you'll hear Reiki music as you're writing your journal or your book if you do and look over your shoulder like I just did and see a woman in an angel outfit looking towards the heavens. And THAT is your message as

"You are and always will be held by angels"

as I was and by loved ones. And you'll take a quick picture as I did of the butterfly, and that will be your affirmation of being protected and loved, and they are maybe reading these last words as you type in 'Stephen King Terriority', and you'll be amazed at how quickly you soak up life and words and po-etry and that you **have started to become** and *are* becoming and just a week ago you get nominated for a Pushcart Prize and you haven't even had the time to tell them because you're still writing and now you are.

"Guess what, babes?"

and they reply,

"I know, darling, don't stop now."

And you don't, you don't, you really just don't.

And all these words are what have made you this story, and it is yours, and it was theirs, and it will always be the way you told your story and spoke your tale, with them and with theirs. Your grief. And that it should be good. And that you maybe chat with them and yourself, your dialogue with Death and Life, that was and is Your Life. And those words you say to yourself about that will, I hope, be

"You are and will be able."

And

"Go on, girl. You got this."

Because you have, you have, you have.

・・•・•・・・

Afterword – Grief – Help and Support Links

Although I have a background in counselling – I am not currently practising as a one-to-one counsellor (2022)– However, I do and can offer support. I am a trainer and facilitator and offer support in other ways.

····•··•····

On my website, there are the weekly 'Grief Writing Workshops'. These are open to those wishing to begin creative grief writing for themselves. Six weeks and longer if required. This can also be offered online by email, for those that are not quite ready to be with other people. The workshop material is then undertaken in your own time. Workshops started in Nov 2022 and are ongoing throughout the year 2023- https://

www.tishincepoetwriter.com/workshops I can be contacted by email at info@tishincepoetwriter.com

Grief Writing Workshops with
Tish Ince Writer

· · • • • • • · ·

I am offering the following links to support organisations in the UK and the US for people experiencing grief and loss:

UK Support
British Association for Counselling and Psychotherapy

https://www.bacp.co.uk/
Cruse Bereavement

https://www.cruse.org.uk/get-support/refer-ring-cruse-faqs/

Widowed and Young

https://www.widowedandyoung.org.uk/

Bereaved by a Brain Tumour Facebook support group -

https://www.facebook.com/groups/219692455100855/

Families in Grief

https://familiesingrief.org/

Other support UK

I-Sing Choirs

https://www.i-singchoirs.co.uk/

Reiki –

Now available on the NHS

(see article)

https://www.complementaryhealthprofessionals.co.uk/

US Support

Grief and Loss Resources Link (Lots of them)

American Association of Counselling

https://www.counseling.org/knowledge-center/mental-health-resources/grief-and-loss-resources

The Centre For Prolonged Grief

https://prolongedgrief.columbia.edu/for-the-public/complicated-grief-public/overview/

About The Author

A Poet - A Writer - A Widow -

Tish Ince is a Trinidadian / Irish London feminist writer and Bay Area published poet. She has a background in youth and community work, person-centred counselling and theatre. This is her debut book - A dramatic memoir of her early grief years and grief journey, the inspiration for her one-woman show, 'This Shite Grief,' and has taken four years to write.

She writes poetry on oppression, anti-racism themes and was nominated for Gloucestershire Poet Laureate, UK, in 2019. She also won a 2020 Paper Nations Marginalised Writer Award South West of England, and in 2022, was nominated for a Pushcart Prize – 'Best of The Small Presses' - Brownstones Poets (New York) for her grief / Ukraine war poem,' I Polish Shoes.' She reads poetry and excerpts from her books globally across Zoom and live events from her San Francsico home.

·········

She began writing her book Good Grief Please! – A Dialogue with Death and Life after the death of her husband, David, in 2017. Her profound experience of grief, complicated grief, and processing her progress along the five stages of grief are met with a 'connection' with her loved ones in spirit and the help and insights they give her along the way.

·········

She is her authentic self in grief, both as a writer capturing the truism of her widowhood no matter how that comes. This is explicit in its pain and profanity, and she warns that she swears throughout though is apologetic for any offense.

She has a number of publications that she is working on including, 'The San Francisco Story,' - her debut poetry collection 'Becoming' – 'On Grief - WIDOWLAND' - A Grief Poetry Collection' - 'On Women' - Poems To Men - Feminist Poetry and 'On War and Poems for Peace'

Tish Ince facilitates Grief Writing - Method Writing and Teen Writers Workshops online at her website and also drops into creative writing spaces: Writers Drop in - The San Francisco Writing Institute, Bay Area BIPOC Writers workshops and in the UK at LIFE Writes – Old Diorama Arts Centre, Euston.

·········

She is a mother to one daughter and grandmother to three grandchildren and lives in San Francisco with her beat poet /publisher and 'alive husband' Dane.

Tish Ince Poet Writer

www.tishincepoetwriter.com

Tish Ince can be contacted by email at

info@tishincepoetwriter.com

Also By Tish Ince

Books and Poetry by Tish Ince

Coming Soon - The San Francisco Story – Published Feb
14th 2023 / Becoming – An Anthology of Poems / On
Grief- Widowland Poems
The Black Widow – A Novel / Widow Dating - A Novel /
On Women – Poems To Men / On War – And Poems For
Peace
Check for more at www.tishincepoetwriter.com

**Scan the QR code on the left to go to Tish Ince Website
| Scan the QR code on the right to go to Tish Ince
Linktree and Socials**